CONTENTS

FOREWORD

This book has been written to those who have been told that God's children should go first-class but have been riding coach...to those who are struggling to keep their Volkswagen on the road but are told they should be riding Cadillacs...to those who are trying to make ends meet in a world whose economy has gone topsy turvy...to those who have been told that God wants them prosperous but so far have only seen the wicked prospering and the ungodly increasing in riches (Psalm 73)...to those caught in circumstances too overwhelming to understand, like Joseph locked up in prison for a crime he did not commit...to those who may be ill and have prayed in faith and made innumerable positive confessions but have not received their healing...and to those who have asked, Why sickness? Why pain? Why sorrow?

This book is also written to those who are enjoying a measure of prosperity and think it's God's guarantee...to those who are not feeling the pinch of poverty or seeing the shadow of sickness and who think their positive confessions are responsible.

Job believed that his uninterrupted success and blessings were a result of his righteous living, and he was right. But then his uninterrupted success was interrupted for reasons that Job could not understand.

Job's guide to survival was trusting God despite his circumstances. Our guide to survival is the same.

This book presents the balance found in God's Word concerning poverty, prosperity, sickness, healing, and God's will.

—Joe Magliato

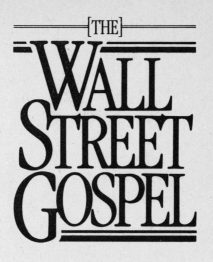

[THE] WALL STREET GOSPEL

Joe Magliato

1
THE WALL STREET
GOSPEL

Suppose you are entertaining friends, and one of them finds his way into your bathroom, notices some mildew growing in the corner of your shower, and then comes out to accuse you of being under a curse.

FRIEND: Marge, do you know you have mildew in your shower?

MARGE: Oh! I'll have to take care of that tomorrow.

FRIEND: Don't you know that mildew is part of the curse of Deuteronomy?

MARGE: Curse? What curse?

FRIEND: The curse of the law. It's all in Deuteronomy 28. But you have been redeemed from the curse.

MARGE: I have?

FRIEND: Yes, you don't have to put up with that. Rebuke it!

MARGE: Rebuke what?

FRIEND: Rebuke the mildew.

MARGE: The mildew?

FRIEND: Yes, all you need to do is to claim your freedom from the curse and believe the Word. If you have enough faith, you won't have mildew in your shower. Don't you have faith?

MARGE: Why sure I do! At least enough to handle mildew.

FRIEND: Maybe you have a secret sin in your life. Is there anything you are hiding?

MARGE: Well, now that you mention it, I did get angry with Bob for knocking over my new geranium pot the other day. But do you think that would be part of the curse?

FRIEND: What do you mean?

MARGE: Well, Bob got so angry when he knocked over the pot that he cursed. Does that count?

FRIEND: You're not taking this seriously, are you?

MARGE: I sure am. It cost me $5.95 for a new pot of geraniums.

FRIEND: Let's believe God to remove the mildew by praying in faith.

MARGE: Why pray? I'll just use "Fungus Sure Shot" first thing in the morning.

Does that sound silly? Well, this logic is used on many Christians who are not fortunate enough to have a lot of this world's goods and are considered living under the curse of poverty. It is bad enough that a fellow brother or sister is struggling to make ends meet without being put under the double burden of living in guilt and condemnation because he is supposed to have faith for prosperity.

There is a strange teaching going around that tells us that material prosperity is our guarantee when we get saved. This teaching tells us we have been freed from poverty, and that we should be driving Cadillacs instead of Volkswagens. The speaker might even take out his Cadillac keys and wave them around with the words, "Go first class—you're a King's kid." He might take out a few large bills, wave them before his audience, and say, "You can't lose with the stuff I use; God wants you to enjoy prosperity."

We are told that we can serve God and get rich. In fact, God wants us to be prosperous. The more prosperous we are, the more glory God gets. I can imagine someone listening to this line of reasoning and thinking to himself, "Well, get out of the way and let me be an instrument to bring God lots of glory while I get the gravy."

We are told, "It's all in the Bible. All you have to do is think God's thoughts, claim it, and it's ours. It's just as easy as that."

Obviously this has lots of appeal, especially for people who are looking for and believing that there must be some shortcut to the American dream. This is not the gospel that we read about in the New Testament, but the gospel according to *Fortune* magazine, the gospel according to Wall Street, Madison Avenue, and the prosperity seekers. It's the gospel that teaches, "Ye shall know them by their Cadillacs." This teaching not only dangles the carrot of riches before people but tells them that God wills their prosperity. In addition to that, if they are not prospering it is because they are under the curse and outside the will of God.

What does the Bible have to say about all this?

If there is an area in which I feel expert, it is poverty. I majored in it while growing up. Dad died when I was seven, leaving my mother to raise all four children alone. Thus began my education in poverty.

I was brought up on the Lower East Side of New York City, a section considered a depressed area. Five of us lived in a 2½-room cold-flat apartment. We were so poor that if a pickpocket put his hand into my pocket all he got was exercise! I wish there had been a war on poverty when I was growing up. I would have walked into a federal building and surrendered. I look back at it now and smile, but going through it was no fun. If anybody is against poverty, I think I stand with the most vocal groups.

When I hear people say that being redeemed from the curse of the law means that we are freed from poverty, I want to stand up and shout, "Amen! Why not?" But I cannot find justification to support the idea that God guarantees material prosperity to His redeemed children.

Let me show you what I find. Paul wrote the

Epistle to the Philippians while in a Roman jail. There was nothing first-class about that rat-infested subterranean cell. It was cold, damp, dark, and foul-smelling. When the sewage water would rise up to his knees, Paul was in want. When you are wet and want to be dry, and you can't do anything about it, you are in want.

Paul did not pace the floor, rebuking the prison and calling on God to "Get me out of here!" Instead of insisting that God send an earthquake or an angel to deliver him, Paul writes:

> I am not saying this because I am in need, for I have learned to be content whatever the circumstances. I know what it is to be in need, and I know what it is to have plenty. I have learned the secret of being content in any and every situation, whether well-fed or hungry, whether living in plenty or in want. I can do everything through Him who gives me strength. *(Philippians 4:11-13)*

Didn't Paul know he was freed from poverty and want? How could he say he is going to be content with want, if all he needed to do was to claim his prosperity?

Why should he have to learn to cope with the curse of want? Why didn't he take authority over the situation by saying, "I don't have to put up with this. I rebuke it. I'm a King's kid!"?

This Wall Street gospel was foreign to Paul. His source was Jesus. Neither wealth nor poverty was his goal or desire. He said that regardless

13

of wealth or poverty he could "do all things through Christ, who strengthens me."

Someone may ask, "Doesn't the Bible say that Jesus became poor that I might become rich? Isn't this my ticket to prosperity?" Is it? Look at the text:

> For you know the grace of our Lord Jesus Christ, that though he was rich, yet for your sakes he became poor, so that you through his poverty might become rich *(2 Corinthians 8:9)*.

The argument usually goes this way: Jesus did not have a bank account, own a house, or drive a chariot. He admitted He did not have a place to lay His head *(Matthew 8:20)*.

Since Jesus was poor in a material sense, and since the Bible says that through His poverty I might be rich, it stands to reason that the riches I receive are material riches. It sounds logical to conclude that Paul is teaching that I receive material wealth when I become a Christian.

However, if this is what Paul is teaching, we either have a major contradiction in Scripture or else we must conclude that Paul himself wasn't receiving what he said we should receive.

In *2 Corinthians 6:10* (just two chapters earlier), Paul gives us a birds-eye view of his own personal financial statement. He writes that he was—

> . . . poor, yet making many rich; having nothing, and yet possessing everything.

If Paul was teaching in *2 Corinthians 8:9* that

14

we are guaranteed wealth and prosperity when
we get saved, must I assume that Paul himself
was poor because he was a below-par Christian?
What was the matter with Paul? Couldn't he
make a "positive confession of faith" and live
in prosperity?

If Paul says that by Jesus' poverty we become
rich, I want to know why Paul couldn't follow
his own teaching? Why was he poor? Or am I to
assume that Paul contradicted himself?

Hardly. Paul was referring to *an entirely different kind of poverty* in *2 Corinthians 8:9*.

In Philippians Paul describes the transition
from Jesus in the form of God to Jesus in the
form of man:

> Who, being in the very nature God, did not
> consider equality with God something to
> be grasped, but made himself nothing, tak-
> ing the very nature of a servant, being
> made in human likeness. And being found
> in appearance as a man, he humbled
> himself and became obedient to
> death—even death on a cross *(Philippians
> 2:6-8)*.

When the Son of God left His mansion of
glory to become a man, stripped of His heavenly
glory, you are looking at the greatest poverty of
all time.

Suppose you became an ant for 30 years. You
would have to give up your human form and
powers to squeeze into the form of an ant. This
process is somewhat parallel to what Jesus experienced when He became a man. The Son of

15

God became the Son of man so that we, the sons of men, might become rich sons of God. That is true riches. The "rich" of *2 Corinthians 8:9* is not *material* riches but *spiritual* riches.

God's Welfare Program for the Poor

God had a welfare program for the poor established long before the children of Israel entered into the Promised Land. This assistance for the poor was to be in operation in the "land flowing with milk and honey."

Farmers were instructed to leave some of their crops in the field unharvested. The poor were allowed to come and take what they needed to keep body and soul together *(Leviticus 19:9,10)*.

At the end of every third year, special food grants and privileges were given to the poor *(Deuteronomy 14:28,29)*. God said the poor would never cease from the land, and that therefore Israel was responsible for showing love and kindness to them *(Deuteronomy 15:1-11)*.

Why would God create laws to care for the poor if they were all cursed?

If God curses something, He does not want us blessing it. King Saul was sent on a mission to destroy the Amalekites. He was to destroy everything that breathed, including the sheep and oxen. When the prophet Samuel wanted to know why King Saul disobeyed God's orders, Saul said that he kept the sheep to offer them to the Lord as sacrifices.

How can Saul take what God has cursed and

16

expect to offer these cursed animals to God as a sacrifice, when to obey meant to destroy what God had cursed *(1 Samuel 15)*?

When the rich or poor sinned, they were required to offer a sacrifice to make atonement for their sins. However, the poor man's sacrifice was based on his ability and means.

A poor man was only required to offer two turtledoves or two young pigeons as a sacrifice *(Leviticus 5:7)*.

Some will argue that this provision for the poor man was an example of God's mercy. Just as a father does not disown a disobedient son, so God does not abandon His children just because they are cursed with poverty.

With this in mind, let us look at a New Testament passage, *Luke 1:28*, in which the virgin Mary is chosen by God to bring Jesus into the world.

God calls Mary "blessed." According to *Deuteronomy 28:4*, a *blessed person* would have offspring.

When Mary visited Elizabeth while still pregnant with Jesus, Elizabeth, filled with the Holy Spirit, said:

> Blessed are you among women, and blessed is the child you will bear! *(Luke 1:42)*.

If Mary was blessed, why is it that she had to offer a poor women's sacrifice when she brought Jesus to the temple to be dedicated *(Luke 2:24)*?

Mary was poor, yet God called her blessed.

17

How could she be blessed while "cursed" in poverty?

If the teachers of the "poverty-is-a-curse" doctrine hesitate to call the virgin Mary cursed when God called her blessed, we do well to think twice before we belittle a poor man's lot in life by assuming that he is poor because he is cursed.

He who mocks the poor shows contempt for their Maker . . . *(Proverbs 17:5).*

Paul was not rich by this world's standards *(1 Corinthians 4:11)*, but I am not about to say that he was poor because he was cursed. Not Paul! You can talk to me about somebody else, but don't tell me Paul was poor because he was cursed or because he lacked faith to rise above his low estate or because he was living below his means.

Paul was a man who exercised faith. He flashes through the New Testament like a streak of lightning with a power that commands attention. When Paul writes, ". . . poor, yet making many rich; having nothing, and yet possessing everything" *(2 Corinthians 6:10)*, that man was not poor. He was throbbing with God's prosperity, even though he didn't have a gold-plated chariot or a fat bank balance.

There were many men of God blessed with material riches. Job, Abraham, David, and Solomon were wealthy men. But we cannot take these individuals and their prosperous lot in life and call it God's ordained pattern for everyone. We need to remember the *other* men

18

of God who did not know where their next meal was coming from. Elijah had to eat food provided for him by a poor widow. Paul earned his expenses by stitching tents. No one had a problem dispensing with Paul's "estate'" when he left this world behind! Peter and John had to tell a lame man, "Silver and gold have I none" *(Acts 3:6 KJV)*. The writer to the Hebrews, describing some of the old-time greats in God's hall of fame, said, "They went about in sheepskins and goatskins, destitute, persecuted, and mistreated" *(Hebrews 11:37)*.

These men of God did not have money. They were not sporting the latest chariot. It could not be said of them, "Ye shall know them by their chariots."

I see nothing wrong with owning the latest chariot, or two of them. If God has allowed us the privilege of wealth, thank God for it and use it as Paul described in 1 Timothy 6:17-19.

But we have no right to impose condemnation on another brother in the Lord who is poor by implying that he is living under the curse.

There were Christians in Jerusalem who suffered want because of hard times. Paul was grateful to those who were willing to contribute to "the poor among the saints in Jerusalem" *(Romans 15:26)*.

Who would read into this text that these saints were poor because they lacked faith to claim material prosperity? Who would argue that the widows of Acts 6 were poor because they were all cursed?

Jesus drew attention to a poor widow woman

in *Mark 12:43,44*. He did not condemn her, but instead *commended* her for giving liberally. If some say that her poverty was a result of her lack of faith, they need to reread this passage. She had so much faith in God that she trusted God totally by giving all that she had. If this is not a display of great faith, I don't know what is. However, we are not told that her great faith was going to be rewarded with great material prosperity. This woman had prosperity in her soul.

These arguments are not presented to teach that poverty is good and prosperity is bad. I am not encouraging poverty. Poverty is not a sign that someone is being blessed any more than prosperity is.

I would no more want poverty than I would start an "I-wish-I-were-poor" campaign. My purpose is to present the balance of Scripture.

I am against the idea of someone waving a diamond ring and flashing car keys around to make people think this is the sign that he is living on the victory side of God's kingdom.

I can show you 50 atheists who will swear at God and wave their rebellious fist at heaven's laws, and still have big diamond rings on their fingers and drive flashy cars, but who are neither blessed of God nor going to His heaven.

Neither prosperity nor wealth is an indication of spirituality. On the other hand, poverty is not necessarily a sign of God's disfavor.

Let those who teach that all the redeemed ought to be and have wealth go to Bangladesh and Cambodia with their teaching on prosperity.

20

Let them preach their Wall Street gospel to the poverty-stricken masses and tell them to claim abundance and material goods. Any gospel that does not work equally well in the Congo or in Chicago is not the New Testament gospel.

The teaching that poverty is a curse and that prosperity is our guarantee is causing frustration and strife among God's people.

A young married man entered ''God's prosperity pact'' with great joy. He began tithing to the church faithfully, expecting God to pour out a financial blessing. He confessed prosperity as he was told and claimed abundance. He listened to the tapes and followed the instructions religiously. His attitude was upbeat and positive.

But after several months I noticed the gathering darkness of discouragement descend over him. He began realizing that what he thought was going to be a simple matter of claiming prosperity was not a simple matter at all. He is still smarting from the false hopes handed to him. His discouragement was compounded when he noticed his non-Christian friends apparently having no problems making ends meet.

Many Christians who are struggling to make ends meet are reaching for the dangling carrot of riches, only to be frustrated. This may then be compounded with despair when they see wicked people prospering. David fell into this trap. He wrote:

I envied the arrogant when I saw the prosperity of the wicked *(Psalm 73:3)*.

It was not until the Psalmist began to see things in the light of eternity that he received a better understanding. After David "entered the sanctuary of God," he understood that God had everything under control, and that in the final analysis God's people would be upheld and those who prospered outside the will of God would meet their just reward *(Psalm 73:17-24)*.

This oversimplified approach of "believe-and-confess" prosperity is misleading. There are roadblocks to prosperity that we need to face squarely.

2
PAINLESS CHRISTIANITY

The American economy thrives on the ability to produce a cheaper model so that it will be easier for more people to purchase, and therefore more items will be sold. If you cannot afford a Cadillac you can always get a look-alike Ford. If you cannot afford a 21-jewel brand name watch you can always get a Timex.

Vinyl, plastic, and artificial veneer take the place of expensive leather, metal, and wood.

Madison Avenue wants to make it easier for us to own their products, and they even give us easy-payment plans. "Relax, you can charge it," they tell us.

The same thing is done in the food industry to make things easier for the housewife. Let her pop the package in the oven and set the dial, and out comes a TV dinner with the instant mashed potatoes and overcooked carrots. The food is precooked, preseasoned, and preheated. It even has extra vitamins and minerals. How much easier can it get? No fuss, no muss, no time, no talent—and of course no taste!

There is a similar philosophy attacking the church today: Make it easier to serve the Lord; make it easier to be a Christian. Attempts are being made to wrap the gospel in an attractive package and advertise it by saying, "We've taken out all the fuss and all the work."

The competition to fill churches is creating a situation in which responsibilities are minimized and privileges are emphasized. When you listen to some of the high-powered TV evangelists you can almost hear them saying, "We will get you to heaven cheaper. Our brand of Christianity is more fun. We make it easier and we don't leave any unpleasant aftertaste. There are no bitter pills to swallow and it won't upset you or your digestive track. Our program is bigger, better, and neater, and it comes with more fringe benefits than any other preacher can give you."

Churches, in trying to make it easier to serve the Lord, are being forced to become more creative in their packaging. "Come in, worship in air-conditioned comfort. Our deacons will meet you at the parking lot to personally chauffeur your car to a parking space (no tipping necessary). And for a dollar or two our deacons will assign a crew to wash and wax your car while you wait and worship. Our pastor is so broadminded that you will never get upset with his messages. He'll get you in and out painlessly. His sermons will pep you up, calm you down, and clean you out, but they won't disturb your conscience. We make it easy, with no obligation, no commitment, no responsibility, no change of lifestyle, no discipline, no repentance, and no growth. We make it cheap and easy.''

Painless Christianity is the Wall Street gospel. But you can't take the cross or the cost out of Christianity and still have the gospel that Jesus died for.

The Cost

Christianity cost God His Son. It wasn't cheap or painless. The shadow of the cross falls front and center.

Christianity is so demanding that we will spend an entire lifetime fulfilling its obligations. We become a debtor to all men. We carry the world on our shoulders. Christianity taxes our every waking hour. It colors our entire outlook. It affects our thinking, our family, our business, and our future. It costs us dearly. Jesus said:

. . . If anyone would come after me, he must deny himself and take up his cross daily and follow me. For whoever wants to save his life will lose it, but whoever loses his life for me will save it *(Luke 9:23,24).*

We handle the cross like a charm or an ornament. We gift-wrap it and pass it out as a present. But Jesus had death in mind when He spoke of the cross. Becoming a Christian always costs and always involves a cross.

25

To one scribe who wanted to join Jesus' group it meant a heavy price. Jesus had to tell him:

"Foxes have holes and birds of the air have nests, but the Son of Man has no place to lay his head" *(Matthew 8:20)*.

To another man who wanted to climb aboard but asked for a leave of absence to wait until his father passed away, Jesus replied that the dead should bury their own dead *(Matthew 8:22)*. To a rich young ruler whose wealth was keeping him from God, following Jesus meant liquidating everything and giving it all away. Coming to Jesus often brings a painful cross.

What will it cost you?

You may have to change your major in college. You may have to rearrange your plans to suit God's will. You may have to postpone your engagement. You may have to break off a friendship, miss a rung up the ladder of success, turn down a promotion, or put an end to a cherished grudge. When a young man (or woman) accepts Jesus, he automatically narrows his field of choices and chances for marriage. There is a price tag and there is a cross.

For Stephen it meant that he would never retire and watch his grandchildren grow up. He was stoned to death. For James it meant an early grave, when King Herod had him beheaded. For Peter it meant that he would never become that wealthy fisherman he had hoped to be. For Paul it meant that he would never spend his twilight years in a Hebrew university but instead in a cold, dark, damp dungeon in Rome. There is always a cross.

But the Wall Street gospel tries to prescribe Christianity with painkillers, to take out the sting, the self-denial, the discipline.

No Cross, No Growth

Too often people join a church and discover that there is discipline, pain, and death of self involved. So they look for another church that caters to their natural desires, a church that emphasizes the power of the resurrection but minimizes the pain of the cross.

God's Word will expose our sin nature, our stubborn streak, our spirit of rebellion, and our temper, jealousy, unforgiveness, bitterness, resentment, and pride. We will begin to feel very uncomfortable under the light of Jesus' teaching. Why? Because the message of the cross demands that we nail these expressions of the old nature on the cross. This is painful.

Instead of surrendering to Jesus, instead of throwing in the white towel and denying self, we slip out of our seat and move our membership to another church. We hide in the back row, lost in the crowd, and try to avoid the discipline and demands of the Word.

We don't want to die to self. It is too painful.

However, a seed must fall to the ground and die if it is ever to grow, and there is no fun in dying.

Isn't there any way I can have the power without the suffering? No! There is no crown without the cross.

The demand of the carnal nature is, "Give us a Christianity that appeals to the flesh; we want our Christianity with painkillers."

Well, we have it. Madison Avenue tactics are being used. A Wall Street gospel has been selling and winning converts by the thousands.

Jesus describes the tragic results of those coming to Him for the excitement and thrill:

What was sown on rocky places is the man who hears the word and at once receives it with joy. But since he has no root, he lasts only a short time. When trouble or persecution comes because of the word, he quickly falls away *(Matthew 13:20,21)*.

Prayers for Sale

We Americans demand instant service. When we step on the accelerator we expect the car to move out. When we turn on the television we expect an instant picture—we don't want to wait around for 30 seconds while the picture tube warms up; we want it now.

And we want our religion to keep pace with our pell-mell race through life. We even try to do this with prayer: "Lord, I want patience and I want it right now."

The Americanized Wall Street gospel has subtly convinced us that we can buy God's blessing and God's answers to prayer. We have been subtly taught that everything has a price tag, so why not answers to prayer too? We receive appeal letters and fund-raising mail that

28

hints, suggests, and implies that we can pay for prayers.

The hints are sprinkled throughout the appeal letters by connecting these two thoughts: 1)We want to pray to take care of your needs; 2)We need your money to take care of our needs. At the end of the computerized letter there are two spaces. Space number one: Send your check or money order. Space number two: List your prayer needs here. The suggestion is subtly and effectively deposited in the mind.

I can pay for an answered prayer. My need of health, wealth, love, happiness, or almost anything else can be purchased with an offering. "You give us what we need (dollars) and we will give you what you need (answered prayer)."

Thousands of Christians have received a personal (computerized) letter from a prominent TV personality. Look at all he has done: Look at all the TV and radio stations he is on; look at all the buildings he has erected; look at all the cassettes and records and books and tracts he has sold; look at all the souls he is winning for Christ. Surely he is in good standing with God. I'll send ten dollars and he will pray for me. Why should I pray when I can pay? I'll get one of God's top-rated servants to pray for me.

This is the Wall Street gospel, geared for bringing in more dollars and getting more work done. But God's blessings and answers to prayer *are not for sale*. Simon discovered this when he offered Peter money for a gift *(Acts 8:9-24)*.

My gift or your gift to any religious organization

will not twist God's arm to get you added blessings. That is not good Christian doctrine, but pagan theology.

Prayer is not a gadget that we plug in for instant results. Money won't speed God's answers.

Let's learn this truth. The psalmist and the prophets all recorded their disappointment with God's prayer-answering service. They all wanted faster delivery. They all felt that God wasn't moving fast enough. The psalmist wrote:

> Awake, O Lord! Why do you sleep? Rouse yourself! Do not reject us forever. Why do you hide your face and forget our misery and oppression? *(Psalm 44:23,24)*.

The saints of old, like us, had to wait on the Lord. Their prayers were not answered instantly. Don't listen to the voices that suggest instant answers. Daniel had to wait 21 days before the answer to one prayer finally got through to him *(Daniel 10:12,13)*.

Can you imagine someone talking to Moses in the wilderness? He had been wandering around there for ten years leading a flock of sheep, and he still had 30 more years to go in God's training program. Some faith teacher comes along and says:

> Hey, Moses, you've been wandering in this wilderness for a decade now. What you need, brother, is victory over this. Here's what I want you to do: I want you to start

claiming victory. Pray this simple prayer with me in faith believing, and you'll be out of this place in two weeks.

Then this faith teacher proceeds to give Moses one of his little booklets entitled INSTANT SUCCESS STORIES IN THE LIFE OF A PRAYING MAN.

God wasn't through with Moses after ten years. But why did Moses have to stay there for 40 years. Because God could not do what He wanted to do with Moses in 39 years. Like it or not, God answers prayer according to His own time and methods.

The answer will always come, but sometimes the answer is *no* or *wait* as well as *yes* (*2 Corinthians 12:9*). We want everything quick, easy, and now. But the gospel teaches us that the crown comes only after the cross. We cannot take the cross or the pain out of the gospel.

We want to be in the army of the Lord. We join up with all the excitement and thrill of joining a winning cause. We are sent to the quartermaster for a uniform. We are given the helmet of salvation, the breastplate of righteousness. We take them and say, "Thank you, but why do I need a helmet and a breastplate?" We are told, "These will protect you from every dart and attack." We are handed a shield and ask, "What is this for?" "This will protect you," says the quartermaster, "from rocks, missiles, and arrows." We look stunned and ask, "Where am I going with all this?" The quartermaster is just as surprised at us as he

31

answers, "Why, you are going into the battle." He hands us a sword and says, "and this is to defend yourself. It is for fighting the enemy." You say, "Wait a minute—I want to be in the army of the Lord, but I don't want to be fighting in any battles."

This is just what the Wall Street gospel is leading us to believe—that we can be in the army of the Lord without fighting any battles. We want to be overcomers, since this fits in nicely with our self-image, but we don't want anything to overcome. No, that is painful.

We don't mind being known as conquerors, but we don't want to conquer anything. We don't want pain, we don't want suffering, we don't want a cross. We want to be called, we want to be spiritual giants, we want the anointing, and we want to be used of God, but we want no suffering, no pain, no cross.

Check out the Word of God. You will discover that power comes through suffering.

Moses chose to suffer affliction with the people of God rather than to enjoy the temporary pleasures of sin *(Hebrews 11:24-26)*.

There was suffering involved. Moses was called to lead 2½ million Jews. He was a powerful and fearless leader. Miracles leaped from his staff. The Red Sea divided in front of him. Water poured out of rocks before him. But when you read the account you notice that Moses did not rest in his tri-level, air-conditioned home sipping lemonade while reading his fan mail. He suffered at every turn in the road. His leadership was constantly

32

under attack. God called Moses but the people criticized his efforts *(Exodus 5:20-23)*.

They ignored him *(Exodus 6:9)*, questioned his motives, criticized his decisions, misunderstood his dealings, and threatened his life *(Numbers 14)*. His own sister, Miriam, rebelled against his authority and split the congregation *(Numbers 12)*. His own brother, Aaron, undid in one weekend what it took Moses years to build *(Exodus 32)*. Moses suffered. He felt rejected, abandoned, and alone. But out of that suffering came power—power to lead in God's strength.

Mary was privileged to give birth to Jesus, God's Son. She was blessed among women, yet she lived in poverty. The day Mary said yes to God she embraced the cross. The shadow of the cross followed her all the days of her life.

She suffered the whispered stories, the raised eyebrows, the ruined reputation. Who would believe that her child was conceived of the Holy Spirit? Why couldn't God do it in a less controversial way? God's power was released through pain. Christianity has never been an escape. It is a cross.

Take the cross out of Christianity and it makes as much sense as a screen door on a submarine.

The secret of our Christian power is not our good looks, our intelligence, our youth, or our experience. It is the cross.

Paul was a dynamo for God. The way some people talk about faith and prosperity and how God's children ought to go first-class, you would expect Paul to have been traveling by limousine service. Money should have been no problem for Paul, and he should have been in the picture of vibrant physical health. But that's not the picture I find in the Bible. The trail of poverty, the broken body, and the physical setbacks fill the New Testament account of this man. He knew the power of the cross. He wrote to the Corinthians:

> For I resolved to know nothing while I was with you except Jesus Christ and him crucified. I came to you in weakness and fear, and with much trembling. My message and my preaching were not with wise and persuasive words, but with a demonstration of the Spirit's power, so that your faith might not rest on men's wisdom, but on God's power *(1 Corinthians 2:2-5)*.

Everywhere you look you find Paul handicapped, bankrupt, and wrestling with a thorn in his flesh even though he prayed three times to have it removed.

Yet none of these setbacks could slow Paul down. The power of the cross moved through this vessel.

Paul gives us a brief birds-eye view of his long list of setbacks:

> Five times I received from the Jews the forty lashes minus one. Three times I was beaten with rods, once I was stoned, three times I was shipwrecked, I spent a night

and a day in the open sea, I have been constantly on the move. I have been in danger from rivers, in danger from bandits, in danger from my own countrymen, in danger from Gentiles; in danger in the city, in danger in the country, in danger at sea; and in danger from false brothers. I have labored and toiled and have often gone without sleep; I have known hunger and thirst and have often gone without food; I have been cold and naked. Besides everything else, I face daily the pressure of my concern for all the churches. Who is weak, and I do not feel weak? Who is led into sin, and I do not inwardly burn? If I must boast, I will boast of the things that show my weakness. The God and Father of the Lord Jesus, who is to be praised forever, knows that I am not lying. In Damascus the governor under King Aretas had the city of Damascus guarded in order to arrest me. But I was lowered in a basket from a window in the wall and slipped through his hands *(2 Corinthians 11:24-33 NIV)*.

None of these things could hold Paul back. There was a power motivating him. He had an annointing. He could go into a city where the economy was based on immorality, and when he left the city had a recession. He wrote to the church at Philippi that his great yearning was to know the power of Jesus' resurrection and the fellowship of His suffering by becoming like Him in His death *(Philippians 3:10)*.

Too many of us would reach for the power of His resurrecton but try to leave out the sharing in His suffering. But the power of Christ's resurrection comes only by way of the fellowship of His suffering—the cross.

Paul was physically weak, but wherever he went the demons trembled. They as much as said, "If you are moving in, we are moving out." He was handicapped, by our standards—he had no printing press, no advance advertising, no modern transportation, and no radio and television—but he was out to win his world for Christ.

Paul's enemies beat him to a pulp and threw him into jail, but he converted the jailer *(Acts 16:16-34)*. They stoned him in Lystra and left him for dead, but the power was there to lift him. He got up, dusted himself off, and went right back to finish his sermon *(Acts 14:19-22)*.

Caesar put Paul in jail. Surely this would silence him. But Paul began converting Caesar's household. There he was holding Bible studies near the king's palace *(Philippians 4:22)*!

Paul was consumed with the message of Jesus' love, and all this through suffering. Before Ananias was sent to pray for Paul, God told Ananias that Paul was scheduled to suffer many things for His cause *(Acts 9:16)*. Paul had power because he knew what it meant to pick up his cross.

This does not mean that if we are not presently suffering for Christ we must be deficient Christians. Not necessarily. Our religious liberty

36

has been protected by our government and we have enjoyed good favor and peaceful circumstances, for which we are thankful. We are not advocating self-inflicted suffering, but we must remember the balance of God's Word.

Peter said:

> You are a chosen people, a royal priesthood, a holy nation, a people belonging to God, that you may declare the praises of Him who called you out of darkness into His wonderful light (*1 Peter 2:9*).

The trouble with too many of us is that we stop at this encouraging word and demand a painless Christianity of nothing but joy. The same Peter who wrote these lines went on to tell the church:

> To this you were called, because Christ suffered for you, leaving you an example that you should follow in His steps (*1 Peter 2:21*).

Keep the balance in your life, and neither pleasant circumstances nor adversities will move you!

3
ROADBLOCKS
TO PROSPERITY

When I was a boy I used to shine shoes to earn spending money. Every Saturday I would get my folding chair and shine box and go down to the subway station to set up my business—shining scuffed shoes. On one occasion after a customer gave me a dollar tip, I knew I was rich. I folded up my chair, picked up my shine box, and headed for the nearest candy store with the attitude that I had the world by the tail. I have since learned the value of a dollar!

However, in Jesus' day the rich people could fit any one of us today. We are rich beyond the wildest dreams of most men on earth. Two hundred years ago the average life expectancy in America was 27 years. At 45 you were old. Today life begins where it used to end 200 years ago. Our homes are palaces compared to the mud-and-stone homes of Jesus' day, and we have an army of mechanical maids at our fingertips.

All we need to do is turn a dial, flip a switch, and twist a knob. The people whom Jesus met would gladly have traded places with us. We are fabulously wealthy.

There is nothing wrong with wealth. It is not a sin to be prosperous. Abraham, you will notice, was not on the welfare roll. Isaac, Jacob, and Joseph were not standing in the bread line either. Many of God's servants were wealthy. Jesus never condemned wealth, but He taught us to handle it with extreme care. Money can become radioactive and eat into our soul. Jesus knew that sometimes, when it comes to riches, we don't own it, but it owns us, and this can be fatal spiritually.

Jesus told the story of the rich fool in *Luke 12:15-21*. He made money hand-over-fist, but there was no scandal connected with his success. He made it fair and square. He was blessed with a string of bumper crops. But God called him a fool. Why? Because he had a fool's idea of security. His trust was in his riches. His one fatal mistake was that he forgot God. He lived as if this world and its goods were all there was. But God said that this was foolish and that any prosperity that pushes God out of the picture is dangerous.

There is a theology going around today that teaches that when we become Christians we are freed from poverty and are candidates for material prosperity. All we need to do is to speak prosperity and abundance. I wish the process were as easy as claiming it and watching prosperity pour in.

40

Consider the reasons that prosperity is not always in the best interest of God's children.

God Will Not Honor Greed

The prodigal son read the devil's advertisement about the far country.

It was alluring—a broad new road to vanity fair. He took his inheritance and lived in prosperity and style. The accommodations were first-class all the way. But this riotous living couldn't last. God waited until the prodigal son had spent all his inheritance and was sitting in a pigpen in desperate poverty.

Poverty turned out to be a blessing for the prodigal son because it brought him to his senses. It was in the pigpen that he decided to get up, get out, and go back to his father's house *(Luke 15:18)*.

His greed and lust were aptly described by Paul when he wrote to Timothy that riches so often result in temptations and desires that plunge men into ruin *(1 Timothy 6:9)*. The prodigal is one example of this kind of deterioration. In this same passage Paul warned that some people even throw their faith overboard because of riches.

The prodigal son was lured into the far country only to discover that it was the land of shattered dreams, disillusionment, and moral bankruptcy.

God does not honor greed as a motivation for material prosperity. Since greed is evil, why should God feed it? When God sees greed and covetousness, His remedy is not prosperity.

41

God prescribes something that kills greed on contact. Jesus prescribed this to the rich young ruler when He told him to go and sell everything he had and then give it to the poor *(Matthew 19:21).*

That is God's answer to greed. God's promises are not given to us in order to build our own kingdoms. If we have been asking but not receiving, we need to examine our motives *(James 4:3).*

God Will Not Honor Theft

Here is another good reason why God will not make a person prosperous: God does not approve of robbery. Anyone enjoying prosperity who is not giving the Lord His tithe is not receiving that prosperity with God's approval *(Malachi 3:8-10).*

Tithing is not intended to be a device to manipulate God. It is not an investment-package deal to finance our way to the top. To be motivated in this way will call forth God's remedy for greed. If tithing were presented in the Bible as a way to realize a greater return for our money, then a Christian who practiced tithing could sue his church if the financial blessing did not come as promised. As a pastor, I would not be so misleading as to guarantee financial rewards for tithing. God will not bless selfish motives. He will, however, bless the motive of love that is willing to give.

So often we hear people referring to Philippians 4:19 as proof of God's desire to bless us with prosperity:

And my God will meet all your needs according to His glorious riches in Christ Jesus.

What was the occasion for this assurance? The context shows that Paul had received a generous gift from the Philippian church. Their unselfish giving would be the basis for God to meet their needs generously. To take this passage and make it guarantee prosperity for all of God's children produces a contradiction in the text. Paul said in Philippians 4:11,12:

I have learned to be content in whatever circumstance I am. I know how to get along with humble means, and I also know how to live in prosperity; in any and every circumstance I have learned the secret of being filled and going hungry, both of having abundance and suffering need (NASB).

If Paul had learned how to be in want, how could he also be saying that God was committed to making us all prosperous?

We need to ask ourselves these questions: Do we know how to live with prosperity? Do we know how to live with poverty?

What have we really learned? If we suffer want, we complain. If we enjoy prosperity, we shift our trust from the Lord to our bank account. Riches take our eyes off Jesus, and poverty drives us to complain.

Paul learned how to cope with want and abundance because his security was not in these things but in Jesus. Whether Paul had much or

43

little, he did all things through Christ, who was his source.

If going through a lean period throws us into a panic, we can be sure we are in bondage to material things. We have not yet learned what Paul teaches in Philippians.

The prophet Habbakuk expressed real prosperity, a prosperity that did not hinge on the Dow Jones averages or anything material.

Though the fig tree does not bud and there are no grapes on the vines, though the olive crop fails and the fields produce no food, though there are no sheep in the pen and no cattle in the stalls, yet I will rejoice in the Lord, I will be joyful in God my Savior *(Habakkuk 3:17,18)*.

God Will Not Honor Mismanagement

God expects us to be good stewards of the possessions we have. When Solomon said that we should honor the Lord with our substance *(Proverbs 3:9,10)*, he was not referring to the tithe. The tithe is not our substance, for it is already God's. God wants me to honor Him with what I have left over after tithes.

I am responsible for the wealth, possessions, and opportunities I have. They are not mine to do with as I please, but to glorify the Lord. I will give an account for the way I manage what I have.

Jesus leaves us with this sense of responsibility in His parable of the talents *(Matthew 25:14-30)*. The servant who received one talent and hid it in the ground was not rewarded for his mismanagement. His one talent was taken and given to the servant who doubled his investment. God expects us to be good custodians of what has been entrusted to us.

God Will Not Honor Lopsided Values

There is another consideration to take into account when we look at prosperity. Jesus said in Matthew 6:19,20:

Do not store up for yourselves treasures on earth, where moth and rust destroy, and where thieves break in and steal. But store up for yourselves treasures in heaven, where moth and rust do not destroy, and where thieves do not break in and steal.

The Lord is concerned with our priorities. He will not honor wrong values. Wrong values may lead some people to great prosperity and possessions, but misplaced values will also result in the loss of the most priceless possession of all—the human soul *(Luke 9:25)*.

We live in an age of *things*. We surround ourselves with things. We sit in expensive things, sleep in expensive things, and drive in expensive things. We have things for the summer, things for the winter, big things, little things, short things, and tall things. We have electrical things, wind-up things, and battery-operated things. Then we have to put locks on these things to secure them against thieves! Most of these things eventually wind up in the garage and then in a garage sale.

45

Things or Relationships

We Americans have this crazy notion that if we own things, we have prosperity. We own cars, boats, motorcycles, homes, cabins, and a long list of other things that all rust and wear out, or fall apart and end up as junk. Real prosperity is not in *things* but in *relationships*. Husband, love your wife! Cherish her with a manly and unalterable affection. That is prosperity!

Wife, do you want prosperity? Love your husband with a godly love and submit to him. The more you love your mate, the more prosperity you are going to enjoy. That relationship is for life. Love your child. Sneak up on her, pick her up off the ground, sweep her into your arms, and tell her "I love you." Spend time with that little bundle of energy that God put into your home. That is prosperity. The things that really count are relationships. Our relationship with God is forever.

We can also enjoy the things that God has created. The Word of God tells us that God has created all things for our enjoyment *(1 Timothy 6:17)*. This earth is a fabulous treasure house. If our eyes could only see the things that ought to be cherished, we would be stepping on the threshold of prosperity.

So often we rush from our home to the office, fighting traffic jams and angry drivers, just to punch our time card, put in our 40 hours, and bring home a paycheck. The vicious cycle has trapped us. Meanwhile time is rushing by and we are overlooking the wonderful people that God has put into our family and circumstances.

We can get so lost on the treadmill of things and trinkets that our only ambition is to grab a fistfull of securities and claim ownership as we take our last breath in the coronary unit. There is nothing wrong with security, but to struggle for it at the expense of losing the precious things we have—our wife, husband, children, friends—is a bad bargain indeed.

Prosperity is to be able to hug your children, to laugh and play with them, to watch them grow, to see them through the chicken pox, and to help them put together a model airplane. The years are ticking off one by one. That child will never be his present age again. Love your children and grow up with them. Squeeze every delightful moment out of true living.

Don't Overlook Spiritual Treasure

The Lord has given us servants, and these servants are the fruit of the Spirit: love, joy, peace, patience, kindness, goodness, faithfulness, gentleness and self-control *(Galatians 5:22,23)*. These spiritual servants can help us make life rich and full.

The spiritual promises of God need to be incorporated into our daily living. We are promised that Jesus will someday break through the clouds, and on that day we will shout, ''Goodbye, world, goodbye!'' We will enjoy it when it happens, but this hope does much to lift our spirits right now. The anticipation is exciting. What price tag can be put on this hope?

Eternal life is already flowing through our

47

spiritual veins. Focus in on that reality for a while. Let hope stir your heart. Don't let another day go by without rejoicing that you have eternal life. You possess it, and that is prosperity.

Sins forgiven, a heavenly mansion, the presence of the Lord, the promises of God's Word, the power of the Holy Spirit—these are things that keep our values in perspective. Neither Chase Manhattan nor the Bank of America could write out a cashier's check to cover these promises!

Put the whole world on one side of the ledger (throw in all the gold and silver), and then put eternal life on the other side of the ledger. You get the world for 70 or 80 years, and then it slips right through your fingers because nobody can take it with him. But eternal life goes with you forever; it marches right past the grave into glory, and earth cannot offer anything to compare with that.

Paul warns Timothy to steer away from an undue emphasis on this world's goods. He admonishes Timothy to put that minister under suspicion who equates gain with godliness. Paul declares that godliness with contentment is great gain *(1 Timothy 6:5,6)*.

Paul was not encouraging Christians to go out and claim material prosperity. He said that we do not bring anything into this world and will not carry anything out. If all we had were the necessities, such as food and clothing, we should be satisfied *(1 Timothy 6:7,8)*.

However, Paul is not condemning riches.

48

Instead, he is pointing to the pitfalls. He does not say that it is a sin to be rich. Paul admits that he learned how to enjoy abundance as well as to be in want. He is not associating wealth with wickedness. He is sounding the warning that greed lurks in the wings of prosperity and riches. Paul tells Timothy to warn Christians already possessing wealth:

> Command those who are rich in this pres-ent world not to be arrogant nor to put their hope in wealth, which is so uncer-tain, but to put their hope in God, who richly provides us with everything for our enjoyment. Command them to do good, to be rich in good deeds, and to be generous and willing to share *(1 Timothy 6:17,18)*.

John puts the emphasis where it ought to be:

> Dear friend, I pray that you may enjoy good health and that all may go well with you, even as your soul is getting along well *(3 John 2)*.

John's emphasis was not on material wealth but on spiritual development. The material prosperity that follows spiritual growth will then be properly handled. When our soul pros-pers, greed will not find fertile ground in which to grow. We will put God's kingdom first in our giving. We will manage our wealth in such a way that we will bring glory to the Lord because our values will not be lopsided.

4
FROM WHAT CURSE ARE WE REDEEMED?

Christ redeemed us from the curse of the law by becoming a curse for us, for it is written: "Cursed is everyone who is hung on a tree." He redeemed us in order that the blessing given to Abraham might come to the Gentiles through Christ Jesus, so that by faith we might receive the promise of the Spirit *(Galatians 3:13,14)*.

These verses have been the object of an erroneous teaching, particularly verse 13:

Christ redeemed us from the curse of the law. . .

It is amazing to me how Christians can take a very simple statement by Paul, confuse it with unrelated theology, and arrive at conclusions that neither Paul nor Jesus taught. The erroneous teaching is: BEING REDEEMED FROM THE CURSE OF THE LAW MEANS BEING FREED FROM POVERTY, SICKNESS, AND DISEASE.

The Curse Begins in Eden

Adam and Eve were placed in a garden paradise where they were blessed with everything they would ever need. There was only one restriction placed on them: They could not eat fruit from the tree of the knowledge of good and evil *(Genesis 2:16,17)*. But Satan entered the garden paradise using the camouflage of a serpent and tempted Eve to eat this forbidden fruit. She not only ate it, but gave some to her husband. The results are recorded in Genesis 3. God cursed the ground with thorns and thistles. Man had to work with great difficulty, and woman would deliver children in much pain and sorrow.

These curses are still very much a part of our daily life. The ground is still cursed, man still works by the sweat of his brow, and women still deliver children by travailing in pain. The evidences of the curse are everywhere. Being redeemed from the curse of the law did not eliminate the curse of pain. If God cursed woman with pain in childbearing, why did God not remove the pain when she was redeemed?

Paul gives us some insight. He said that all creation is groaning and travailing in pain. He also states that even the redeemed, those of us who have been redeemed from the curse of the law, those of us who have the firstfruits of the Spirit—

> We ourselves . . .groan inwardly as we wait eagerly for our adoption as sons, the redemption of our bodies *(Romans 8:23)*.

We are groaning because we are waiting. We are waiting for our bodies to become glorified. This transformation is still future. We will receive our glorified bodies as soon as the trump of God shall sound and the dead in Christ shall rise first, followed by those who are alive *(1 Thessalonians 4:16,17)*.

Paul tells us that we will be changed instantly as our mortal bodies suddenly become responsive to the heavenly tug. In a split second of time death will lose what it once had and life will become supercharged with God's full redemptive power *(1 Corinthians 15:51-54)*.

The future aspect of our bodily redemption is not an isolated teaching in Scripture. Paul taught the Ephesians:

> You were marked in him with a seal, the promised Holy Spirit, who is a deposit guaranteeing our inheritance until the redemption of those who are God's possession . . . *(Ephesians 1:13,14)*.

The Ephesians had no problem understanding this analogy. They lived by the water where loggers brought their cut trees. Logging companies would send representatives to purchase the logs. The purchased logs were not taken to the mills on the day of their purchase, but were marked with the owner's seal to wait for their "redemption". Redemption meant the actual taking away of the purchased logs to the mill.

In the same way we have been sealed by the Holy Spirit. We have been purchased "with the precious blood of Christ" *(1Peter 1:19)* and are

53

waiting for the day when we will be completely redeemed.

Jesus looked past Calvary to some future generation and warned that there would be signs occurring in the sun and the moon. The earth would convulse with natural upheavals, and then the Son of Man would suddenly appear in power and great glory, The generation seeing these things should look up because their redemption is drawing near *(Luke 21:28)*.

New Testament theology does not teach that we are completely freed from the physical traces of the curse. John tells us that complete redemption is still future, when God—

> will wipe every tear from their eyes. There will be no more death or mourning or crying or pain, for the old order of things has passed away *(Revelation 21:4)*.

If someone told me that all I needed to do was to accept Jesus and then all the curses brought on by man's fall would suddenly leave, including pain and sorrow, I would be the first in line to sign up. However, it does not take a seminary education to realize that though we are saved there is still plenty of pain and sorrow around for both saved and unsaved people. Death is still a public enemy. Should Jesus tarry, we will die. The statistics and obituary column speak eloquently to this fact. Pain and suffering are obvious manifestations that death is still working. It does not matter how long we have been saved, or how much faith we can generate, or how healthy we are—there is

54

something about our present body that still needs redemption *(Romans 8:23)*.

When does this redemption occur? When I accept Jesus as my Lord and Savior? No. It is scheduled for the new heaven and the new earth. When I receive my new body the curse will be gone. The curses resulting from sin in the Garden of Eden will be with us until we get to the end of Revelation. *(22:3)*. The curses that turned man's utopian existence into a lifelong struggle of pain and sorrow will be lifted in the future, when we are given brand-new bodies.

We have to wait. The redemption is still future. Now, if I am redeemed from the curse of the law, what curse is this?

What is the Curse of the Law?

Therefore, just as sin entered the world through one man, and death through sin, and in this way death came to all men, because all sinned *(Romans 5:12)*.

When Jesus was crucified, the sins of all the world—past, present, and future—were put on Him *(1 John 2:2)*. He "became sin" *(2 Corinthians 5:21)*. He took my guilt, my sin, my hatred, my rebellion, my envy, my temper, my habits, and everything about me that was wicked. It was all nailed to the cross with Him. I no longer face the death penalty since Jesus paid the price. I am redeemed from the curse of the law.

The curse of the law came because of the offense of one man, Adam. His sin brought con-

55

demnation, but redemption came because of the righteousness of one man, Jesus. His righteousness brought justification *(Romans 5:18)*.

Being justified means that God no longer sees me as a sinner. Instead, He sees me as if I had never sinned. Therefore, being redeemed from the curse of the law means that I am no longer under condemnation *(Romans 8:1)*.

The Curse and Curses

Why do some compare the curse of Galatians 3:13 with the curses of Deuteronomy 28? Is there a connection?

When we get to the Book of Deuteronomy, the children of Israel are ready to enter the Promised Land. Forty years of wandering are behind them. Moses gathers them together for a final word of instruction and warning. Deuteronomy 28:15-68 contains a list of curses that would come upon the nation if they refused to obey the Word of the Lord.

The curses were physical punishments for disobeying God. There is no mention of spiritual death, which is the curse of the law in New Testament teaching.

The curses of Deuteronomy 28 are warnings to a nation, not an individual. The curse of the law in Galatians 3:13 is the individual curse that we receive because of sin.

Examine the curses of Deuteronomy 28 and see whether they were intended for individuals or the nation. If every individual who violated

56

God's law received all these curses, we would have a ridiculous situation.

First, for disobeying God's Word, pestilence (a total epidemic) will cling to your body until you die *(Deuteronomy 28:21)*. Then you will die of consumption and a variety of ailments all designed to be terminal *(Deuteronomy 28:22)*.

As if dying several times were not enough, more curses continue to pile up—severe drought, utter defeat in battle, dispersion among the nations, leprosy, tumors, malignant scurvy, insanity, and other horrors, including your carcass becoming food for the birds *(Deuteronomy 28:26)*.

Now simply ask yourself, are all people who break God's law physically sick and diseased? Do they fit the conditions just described above? Of course not. God is speaking to the nation of Israel. If we look at the historical record, we find that these curses actually came to pass nationally. For example, Israel was taken into Babylonian captivity *(Deuteronomy 28:41)*. They were scattered all over the world *(Deuteronomy 28:63-65)*.

If the curses of Deuteronomy 28 were going to fall upon every individual who broke the law of God, then all nonbelievers would be in terrible shape, physically and materially. But we know that this is not the case. We all know wicked people who are not only prospering but are in excellent health. They certainly do not fit the cursed conditions described in Deuteronomy 28.

However, according to the authority of God's Word we know that all wicked people everywhere are under the curse of the law. That curse is guilt, condemnation, and spiritual death. This is the condition of all unsaved people everywhere, whether they are poor or prosperous, physically sick or healthy.

According to the current teaching, poverty is supposed to be the sign that I am living under the curse of the law.

If poverty were the consequence of breaking God's law, we would expect to find it demonstrated throughout Scripture consistently. For example, Lot pitched his tent toward Sodom and began to mingle with the heathen. This obviously was not in keeping with God's will for Lot, because God was getting ready to destroy this city. As a result, Lot ended up living in poverty *(Genesis 19)*.

But we do not see this same sequence of events for David's disobedience when he took another man's wife and had her husband killed. David never suffered the curse of poverty.

If breaking God's law always results in poverty, I need someone to explain why the psalmist complains that the ungodly were prospering and increasing their riches *(Psalm 73:12)*.

If living in sin does not necessarily guarantee that an individual will become poor, then living in Christ does not necessarily guarantee that a person will obtain material prosperity. However, the New Testament does teach that living in sin always means

58

. . .dead in your transgressions and sins *(Esphesians 2:1)*.

and that accepting Jesus as Lord always means being made alive unto Christ.

Then what do the curses of Deuteronomy mean to us? They remind us that disobedience may result in severe consequences. It is not outside God's disciplinary program to use physical punishment for disobedience.

This can be clearly seen in the case of Ananias and Sapphira *(Acts 5)*, and in the punishment prescribed for a backslidden Christian involved in sexual immorality *(1 Corinthians 5:5)*. God has used in the past and will continue to use discipline in training His children *(Hebrews 12:6-7)*.

When Moses spoke these words to Israel, they knew all too well of God's determination to punish disobedience. They witnessed the deaths of their parents in the wilderness because of the unbelief and rebellion *(Numbers 4)*. The curses of Deuteronomy 28 carry a strong warning.

The Blessing and Blessings

Are the "blessing of Abraham" *(Galatians 3:14)* and the blessings of Deuteronomy 28 one and the same?

The blessings of Deuteronomy 28:1-14 are all material blessings. Is the blessing of Abraham material?

The blessing of Abraham is justification

59

through faith. Jesus is the blessing which would bless the nations *(Genesis 12)*.

We have a new and better covenant. This covenant is based on faith in Jesus (Hebrews 8:6-13).

. . .He sets aside the first to establish the second *(Hebrews 10:9)*.

The new covenant no longer places an emphasis on material possessions. A man's wealth does not determine his standing with God.

In addressing Christians who had their personal possessions plundered during persecution, the writer to the Hebrews says:

You. . .joyfully accepted the confiscation of your property, because you knew that you yourselves had better and lasting possessions *(Hebrews 10:34)*.

Here we have an example of the better covenant. The blessing of the new covenant is far better than the blessings under the law.

The blessing of Abraham is Jesus. We receive His peace that passes understanding *(Philippians 4:7)* and His forgiveness without having to continually offer sacrifices *(Hebrews 10:11)*. We have His constant presence through the power of the Holy Spirit within us *(John 14:26)*, and we have His never-ending promises *(Romans 8)*.

The curse of the law is guilt, condemnation, and spiritual death. The blessing of Abraham is Jesus. This is New Testament theology.

We need to study God's Word. It is so easy to

fall prey to false teaching. Peter warned us to steer clear of teachers who appeal to the lustful desires of the sinful human nature *(2 Peter 2:3)*.

False teachers do not wear a sign on their back stating "False Teacher, Beware." They come with sweet and pleasant-sounding words, words that cater to our fallen nature and bring us into spiritual bondage, as we will see in succeeding chapters.

5
WHY PEOPLE GET SICK

We are body, mind, and spirit. Sickness and disease can occur in any one of these areas. When the body's resistance breaks down, sickness and disease take over. Eating junk foods, too many sweets and starches, or too much salt can create malfunctions. The connection between smoking and cancer is undeniable. There are many abuses of the body that can cause sickness.

Besides these obvious abuses, there are mental stresses which can also break down the body's resistance. Medical science has established the tie between emotional stress and the majority of our sicknesses. It is estimated that 80 percent of the hospital beds are filled with people who are there because of emotionally induced illnesses.

Emotions of worry, fear, anger, jealousy, and other stress conditions can cause high blood pressure, migraine headaches, heart trouble, and other serious diseases. Ulcers often occur not so much from what we eat but from what's eating us. Physicians can prescribe medicine for the symptoms of these diseases, but the root cause will not be cured with a pill.

Solomon said that a negative mental attitude will produce physical disease while a cheerful attitude will act as medicine to the body *(Proverbs 17:22)*.

If there are any doubts as to the effect of emotional stress on the body, consider the following:

A five-year-old boy breaks out in hives whenever he has to spend a week with his Aunt Margaret. Investigation shows that her constant nagging and ridiculing bring on the hives.

A business executive complains of migraine headaches whenever he has to meet new clients or attend board meetings.

Consider the last minute you were embarrassed. In a fraction of a second the thought in your mind caused blood vessels in your face and neck to open up and produce blushing and perhaps a nervous twitch.

When we begin to examine emotional upset and stress, we often come to an even-deeper level as a cause. Unresolved spiritual conflicts and sin can produce emotional turmoil. Becoming bitter or rebellious toward God or refusing to trust Him produces insecurity, guilt, fear, and worry, which in turn can result in physical illness.

64

When the lame man in Mark 2 was let down through a roof for healing, Jesus told him that his sins were forgiven *(Mark 2:5)*. Jesus first dealt with his physical problem at the spiritual level, where the real cause of his paralysis centered. Once the spiritual problem (sin) was removed, Jesus would heal the physical condition.

Sometimes the thing standing between us and our healing is unforgiveness. After Jesus encourages us to speak to our mountain of difficulty and to believe that we will receive what we ask, He then instructs us to forgive.

> And when you stand praying, if you hold anything against anyone, forgive him, so that your Father in heaven may forgive you your sins *(Mark 11:25)*.

Apparently our receiving may be held up by our lack of forgiveness.

Some of our prayers may be put on "hold" until we are willing to forgive. Notice that forgiveness and healing often go hand-in-hand:

> He forgives all my sins and heals all my diseases *(Psalm 103:3)*.

The cause for sickness in 1 Corinthians 11:28-30 is spiritual in nature:

> A man ought to examine himself before he eats of the bread and drinks of the cup. For anyone who eats and drinks without recognizing the body of the Lord eats and drinks judgment on himself. That is why many among you are weak and sick, and a number of you have fallen asleep.

65

Paul is warning that neglecting to discern the Lord's body will bring sickness and premature death.

What is discerning the Lord's Body? Here is an example: Your body has ten fingers, two eyes, a nose, a mouth, and other parts. If the members of your body were to begin fighting each other, physical difficulties would occur. If the fingers and fist began scratching the face and punching the body, black and blue markings would appear. If kept up long enough, sickness of some kind would result.

When we relate to our brother or sister in the Lord with strife, backbiting, jealousy, and maliciousness, we are in effect not "discerning the Lord's Body." We will bring sickness on ourselves. If we take good care of our physical bodies, we should also take good care of the Body of Christ, which is the church. We are to be kind and compassionate to the members of His Body *(Ephesians 4:15,16)*.

Discipline and Sickness

Discipline as a cause for sickness is quite unpopular in many circles, and has been considered an unacceptable explanation by many faith ministries. But like it or not, this is the way it is. Sometimes God will allow sickness in order to discipline us.

David sinned against the Lord and was met by the prophet of God, who announced three forms of disciplinary action. David was to choose one:

Shall there come upon you three years of

famine in your land? Or three months of fleeing from your enemies while they pursue you? Or three days of plague in your land? *(2 Samuel 24:13)*

David responded that it would be much better to fall into the hand of the Lord and suffer a plague of sickness and disease *(2 Samuel 24:14,15)*.

Now I am sure a great chorus of protest will rise up saying, "The Lord would never do a thing like this!" But He did, and David remembered the Lord's dealing with him when he wrote:

Before I was afflicted I went astray, but now I obey your word *(Psalm 119:67)*.

Any shepherd knew what this meant. If a sheep strayed away from the flock over and over again, the shepherd would use a slingshot to send out an angry pebble to get a message to that sheep. The shepherd also had a rod and a staff. If the sheep continued his AWOL activities, eventually the shepherd would take his rod and break the sheep's leg. He did this to discipline the sheep and keep it from bringing greater danger on itself. The sheep could say before he was afflicted that he went astray. Affliction can be used to get us back in line. The Psalmist goes on to say that *it was good* that he went through afflictions so that through them he might learn God's law *(Psalm 119:71)*.

You can be sure that as the affliction was being experienced the psalmist would not be saying,

67

"It is good for me." That is why it is in the past tense—"have been afflicted." When the psalmist looked back at this experience he could see what God was accomplishing in his life, and so he said, "It is good."

No discipline seems pleasant at the time, but painful. Later on, however, it produces a harvest of righteousness and peace for those who have been trained by it *(Hebrews 12:11)*.

When God called Moses to deliver the children of Israel from Egyptian bondage, Moses was not in a frame of mind to go. He resisted his calling with a variety of excuses, and among them was this one:

O Lord, I have never been eloquent, neither in the past nor since you have spoken to your servant. I am slow of speech and tongue *(Exodus 4:10)*.

Apparently Moses had a speech impairment, for the Lord's reply indicates this:

The Lord said to him, "Who gave man his mouth? Who makes him deaf or dumb? Who gives him sight or makes him blind? Is it not I, the Lord? *(Exodus 4:11)*.

The Lord promised to cure the defect in Moses' speech:

Now go; I will help you speak and will teach you what to say *(Exodus 4:12)*.

But Moses rejected God's offer to heal him. He

68

insisted on hiding behind his speech defect and asked God to send Aaron, his brother, instead.

We see here a strange set of circumstances. God is implicating Himself in initiating a blindness and dumbness on occasion. I believe that the Scriptures will support God's disciplinary use of both blindness and dumbness.

An angel was sent to Zacharias (Zechariah) to announce the birth of John the Baptist. Zacharias was old and found it difficult to believe that his wife would give birth.

> Zechariah asked the angel, "How can I be sure of this? I am an old man and my wife is well along in years." The angel answered, "I am Gabriel. I stand in the presence of God, and I have been sent to speak to you and to tell you this good news. And now you will be silent and not able to speak until the day this happens, because you did not believe my words, which will come true at their proper time" (Luke 1:18-20).

This is clearly a case in which the Lord initiated speech impairment as disciplinary action. Somewhat similar to this was Paul's experience on the road to Damascus. His intention was to haul Christians off to jail, break up services, and stamp out all traces of Christianity. A light from heaven caused him to fall to the ground. The Lord spoke to Paul, after which he got up from the ground as a blind man.

> Saul got up from the ground, but when he opened his eyes he could see nothing. So

69

they led him by the hand into Damascus
(Acts 9:8).

It is true that this blindness lasted only three
days, but it was three days of disciplinary action. Ananias was sent by the Lord to pray for
Paul after which we read:

Immediately, something like scales fell
from Saul's eyes, and he could see again
(Acts 9:18).

When Elymas the sorcerer tried to prevent Paul
from preaching the gospel to the deputy of the
Isle of Paphos, he became the object of God's
disciplinary action. Paul said,

Now the hand of the Lord is against you.
You are going to be blind, and for a time
you will be unable to see the light of the
sun. Immediately mist and darkness came
over him, and he groped about . . . *(Acts
13:11)*.

It is not outside God's will to use sickness as
punishment. After Naaman was healed of
leprosy *(2 Kings 5)*, he offered Elisha gifts,
which the prophet refused. Naaman started
back to Syria when Elisha's servant, Gehazi,
caught up with the healed captain and con-
cocted a story about an unexpected emergency
arising which would be alleviated if Naaman
contributed a talent of silver and some changes
of clothes.

Naaman responded generously with two
talents of silver and two changes of clothes.

70

When Gehazi returned with his spoil, his scheme was discovered by the prophet Elisha, who said:

Naaman's leprosy will cling to you and to your descendants forever. Then Gehazi went from Elisha's presence and he was leprous . . . *(2 Kings 5:27)*.

Let those who dispute the justice of this punishment take it to God. If God's actions do not fit neatly into our formula, then perhaps we need to change our formula.

Overwork

We find an unexpected cause for sickness in the New Testament. Paul gives us the account of a fellow minister who got sick.

But I think it is necessary to send back to you Epaphroditus, my brother, fellow worker and fellow soldier, who is also your messenger, whom you sent to take care of my needs. For he longs for all of you and is distressed because you heard he was ill. Indeed he was ill, and almost died. But God had mercy on him, and not on him only but also on me, to spare me sorrow upon sorrow. . . .

Welcome him in the Lord with great joy . . . because he almost died for the work of Christ, risking his life to make up for the help you could not give me *(Philippians 2:25-30)*.

71

Epaphroditus became sick because he over-worked. It was neither hidden sin nor a lack of faith. We might ask how a minister of God could get sick when there was so much work to do. Paul gives us some insight in *2 Corinthians 4:16* when he says that outwardly we are perishing while inwardly we are becoming stronger.

We are still waiting for the day when we get our glorified bodies!

Old Age

Our bodies are getting older, and the older they get, the weaker they get. I believe this was Daniel's experience. The aged prophet of God saw a vision and recorded his physical reaction:

> I, Daniel, was exhausted and lay ill for several days. Then I got up and went about the king's business *(Daniel 8:27)*.

Daniel's credentials were impressive. He was a man of God who received many visions and had the gift of interpreting dreams. He also received divine health after proving to the prince of the eunuchs that foods approved by his God would produce startling results. The ten-day trial resulted in this evaluation:

> At the end of the ten days they looked healthier and better nourished than any of the young men who ate the royal food *(Daniel 1:15)*.

Yet in his old age Daniel succumbed to the weakness of his body when he fainted and became sick (from which he recovered). However, although Daniel recovered, Elisha did not recover from his sickness.

Elisha was a man of God who received a double portion of Elijah's spirit *(2 Kings 2:9)*. He performed twice as many miracles as Elijah, but in his old age we read that he was suffering from an illness which was fatal *(2 Kings 13:14)*.

How are we to interpret Elisha's sickness? Did he suddenly have a lapse of faith? If he did, I need someone to explain the following passage of Scripture:

> Elisha died and was buried. Now Moabite raiders used to enter the country every spring. Once while some Israelites were burying a man, suddenly they saw a band of raiders; so they threw the man's body into Elisha's tomb. When the body touched Elisha's bones, the man came to life and stood up on his feet *(2 Kings 13:20,21)*.

This does not sound like Elisha died without faith. If there was something spiritually wrong with Elisha, causing him to die in his sickness, why did his bones retain enough power after his death to resurrect a dead man?

I am not building a case for people to get sick and enjoy it. I am building a case for the reality that there are many reasons for sickness. Healing is a *benefit* and not a *guarantee* of Calvary.

All too often people have made healing a simple matter of "have faith and get healed." That is not what I see in the Bible.

According to the Gospel of John, chapter 11, Lazarus was a sick man.

> Now a man named Lazarus was sick . . . .
> When he heard this, Jesus said, "This sickness will not end in death. No, it is for God's glory so that God's Son may be glorified through it" *(John 11:1,4).*

I do not understand all the whys of God's actions, but I read here that Jesus said that Lazarus' sickness would result in glory to God. We are told that Jesus loved Lazarus.

With a little imagination we can reconstruct this story. Mary and Martha call a healing evangelist who is ministering in the area. The evangelist arrives and engages Lazarus in conversation. "Lazarus, I am going to read some Scripture verses to you in order to build your faith to believe." So the evangelist reads:

> "I am the Lord who heals you" *(Exodus 15:26).*
> "The Lord will keep you free from every disease" *(Deuteronomy 7:15).*
> "He sent forth His word and healed them" *(Psalm 107:20).*

Then the evangelist lays hands on Lazarus, anoints him with oil, and prays. After this he says, "Lazarus, by faith you are healed. God's Word says it and I believe it." The evangelist then turns to Mary and Martha and says, "Don't be worried about anything. Lazarus is healed."

"But he doesn't look healed" Mary says. To

74

this the evangelist replies, "That is a negative confession. I prayed one time and that is all I need to pray. Praying again would mean I doubted that God heard me. Your brother is healed!"

But Lazarus dies. Four days later Jesus arrives and calls Lazarus out of the tomb and back to life.

Now I want you to notice that when Lazarus was in the tomb he had zero faith. Yet he was resurrected—not because he had great or little faith, but because of Jesus' word. However, Jesus predicted that Peter would die for the glory of God, and that there would be no immediate resurrection for him.

Jesus said this to indicate the kind of death by which Peter would glorify God . . . (John 21:19).

I find it unscriptural to arbitrarily tell a brother who is flat on his back that he is sick due to a lack of faith or because he has some hidden sin in his life. There are other explanations.

Jesus is a good authority on the subject of sin, sickness, and lack of faith. When the disciples saw a man born blind, they asked who was responsible for the man's blindness (John 9:2.) Jesus answered, that the man's blindness was not due to either his sin or his parents'.

This man's blindness was not due to a lack of faith, either. Since he was born blind he could not be penalized for a lack of faith. Jesus

75

indicated that God would receive glory through this *(John 9:3)*.

It is true that faith is needed for healing, but we must not overlook the instances in which it is not faith that stands in the way of healing, but confession *(James 5:16)*. In other cases it is neither the lack of faith nor the need for confession, but the Lord working out His divine plan *(John 9, 11; 2 Corinthians 12; Galatians 4)*.

Oversimplifying the subject of healing by saying that all one needs is faith can be very dangerous. Consider the parents who put their faith in the Lord and then removed insulin from their diabetic child, only to see him die. They were charged with manslaughter.*

This teaching has caused some saints to doubt their salvation because they were taught that true children of God are immune from sickness since they are redeemed from the curse of the law. But since they get sick anyway, they assume there is something spiritually wrong with them.

Satan must have a field day with saints who have been caught up in this wind of false doctrine. God's children need to recognize this for what it is. Studying the whole counsel of God will help them recognize a false doctrine when they see it.

Just before leaving for a day at Universal Studios with my wife and children, I put on my sunglasses, turned to my son, and said, "I guess you won't be able to recognize me in these sunglasses." My son answered, "I can recognize you because you're my dad." A pair of sunglasses could not keep him from recognizing his dad.

Christians who know their Lord and study His Word will not be fooled by disguised half-truths or shaded areas. Their knowledge of God's Word will help them recognize the false from the true.

---

* Read *We Let Our Son Die* (Harvest House Publishers).

6
THE MYSTERY OF HEALING

There is a strong emphasis in some circles that insists that no Christian should ever get sick; and if he does, he should be healed immediately by faith. This oversimplified position leaves many of God's people living with a sense of guilt and defeat.

God wants us to be healthy. He gave the church "gifts of healing" *(1 Corinthians 12:9).* We are taught that the prayer of faith can bring about our healing.

> Is anyone among you sick? Let him call for the elders of the church, and let them pray over him, anointing him with oil in the name of the Lord; and the prayer offered in faith will restore the one who is sick, and the Lord will raise him up *(James 5:14,15 NASB).*

It seems from this passage that a sick person needs faith in order to get well. "The prayer of faith shall save the sick." However, standing between us and our healing may not be a need for a prayer of faith but a confession of our faults. James continues to instruct us:

> Therefore, confess your sins to one another, and pray for one another, so that you may be healed *(James 5:16 NASB).*

If our sickness is related to unforgiveness, grudges, resentments, or disobedience, having great faith is not going to bring about a healing.

Some Physical Sickness Is Spiritual In Nature

God wants us to be healthy, but if we violate His spiritual laws we can bring sickness on ourselves *(1 Corinthians 5:5; 11:30).*

I remember a man who developed palpitations of the heart and shortness of breath shortly after his son-in-law ran away with another woman. He was afraid a heart attack was imminent. When he came to the altar for prayer, the Lord said to him, "Forgive your son-in-law." He argued with the Lord that his son-in-law ran away from his daughter and was to blame. Week after week he asked the Lord to heal him, and each time the Lord asked him to forgive his son-in-law.

Finally he gave up and said, "All right, Lord, I forgive him." He was instantly healed. The palpitations of the heart instantly left, as did the shortness of breath. He got up from the altar a healed man. His was a spiritual problem. It

80

was not a lack of faith but a lack of *forgiveness* that kept him ill. Our forgiveness can keep us from God's blessings.

I read of a young lady who was seeking a closer walk with the Lord. While she was praying the Lord impressed upon her to forgive her father. She rebelled from the very thought, because her father had violated her when she was 12 years of age. Why should she forgive him? He was at that moment sitting in a mental institution.

The spiritual struggle continued until she gave in to the Lord's demand and forgave her father. Immediately she was released from within and felt a freedom she had never experienced before.

Two days later she learned that for the first time her father was responding favorably to treatment. The power of forgiveness had set both of them free.

Whose Lack Of Faith?

When someone is not healed after he is prayed for, he may be told subtly or directly that his healing was held up because he did not have enough faith. This pat answer does not always hold up. When the disciples prayed for an epileptic boy and could not deliver him, the matter was taken to Jesus by the boy's father, who said:

I brought him to your disciples, but they could not heal him *(Matthew 17:16).*

The disciples asked Jesus privately why they

could not cast out this demon and were told that their unbelief was the cause *(Matthew 17:20)*. Jesus blamed His disciples. Could it be that there are times when the minister has a problem in the area of faith? Jesus indicates this.

Why is it that we are guilty of giving pat answers to complex problems? We make healing seem like a simple matter of: "A" is sick, "B" prays for "A", God hears and answers. There are mysteries that surround us in the realm of healing that need to be recognized. There is an old church hymn that goes, "We'll Understand It Better By and By." There are some things we do not understand. Wouldn't it be wonderful if everything squared with our simple formulas? Consider this text:

> In this meaningless life of mine I have seen both of these: a righteous man perishing in his righteousness, and a wicked man living long in his wickedness *(Ecclesiastes 7:15)*.

It would be so much nicer if this bit of information did not have to be programmed into the computer of reality. It would be so much simpler if the good guys always wore white hats and came in first, while the bad guys always wore black hats and came in last. However, this is childish. There are mysteries about the justice and mercy of God that we cannot fathom. The prophet Jeremiah asks why the wicked prosper *(Jeremiah 12:1)*. You see, according to his understanding the wicked should have been suffering.

There will come those moments in our lives when our faith is tested to the breaking point and we can only make the affirmation that the Judge of all the earth will do right *(Genesis 18:25)*.

We might as well face it—we live with mysteries, and healing is one of those mysteries.

We are so prone to devise simple formulas in our theology. But under the scrutiny of God's Word these formulas crumble.

At the beginning of the Book of Acts we see what appears to be a formula of salvation. First you repent, and then you get baptized in water, and finally you receive the gift of the Holy Spirit *(Acts 2:38)*. The formula sounds good until we come to Acts 9, where Paul is converted after a blinding-light experience on the Damascus Road.

When Ananias prays for Paul he is healed and then is filled with the Holy Spirit *(Acts 9:17)* and some time later is baptized in water.

When we get to the tenth chapter of Acts, Peter is halfway through his sermon when the power of the Holy Spirit comes upon his audience, and to the astonishment of Peter and his evangelistic party these people received "the gift of the Holy Spirit" *(Acts 10:45)*. After this they were baptized in water.

By this time our simple formula of believe, be baptized in water, and receive the Holy Spirit has crumbled. We can't get the formula to work. Perhaps what we need to do is get rid of some of those formulas and come to grips with the mystery of God's working.

Is Healing A Part Of Our Salvation?

Isaiah 53:4 literally says:

Surely our sicknesses He Himself bore and our pains He Himself carried.

Healing belongs to God's people. God did not create this planet to be filled with diseased bodies. God does not want people sick. He wants us healthy. Jesus' death carries healing for the total man.

When evening came, many who were demon-possessed were brought to him, and he drove out the spirits with a word and healed all the sick. This was to fulfill what was spoken through the prophet Isaiah:

"He took up our infirmities and carried our diseases" *(Matthew 8:16-17)*.

The Greek word for "infirmities" is used as bodily sickness in *John 5:5; Luke 13:11,12; Acts 28:9; and Timothy 5:23*.

As a verb, it is the common word for "being sick" (Luke 4:40; 7:10; John 11:3).

Strong's Exhaustive Concordance defines "infirmity" as malady, disease, sickness, and weakness.

Although Paul saw miraculous healings in his ministry, he confesses to having an infirmity.

As you know, it was because of an illness that I first preached the gospel to you. Even though my illness was a trial to you, you did not treat me with contempt or scorn *(Galatians 4:13,14)*.

In *2 Corinthians 12:5*, Paul again confesses to having infirmities. However, on this occasion Paul tells us that he asked God to remove his infirmity, but that his request for healing was denied. Then Paul writes:

> That is why, for Christ's sake, I delight in weaknesses . . . . For when I am weak, then I am strong *(2 Corinthians 12:10)*.

Instead of claiming deliverance, making a positive confession of faith, and refusing to accept his sickness, Paul accepts his infirmity.

The Scriptures teach that God wants us well, but Paul finds no contradiction in his not being healed. In fact, Paul advises Timothy on one occasion to take medicine for his ill health:

> Stop drinking only water, and use a little wine because of your stomach and your frequent illnesses *(1 Timothy 5:23)*.

Both The Pulpit Commentary and *Vincent's Word Studies in the New Testament* confirm that Timothy's problem was "sickness and attacks of illness."

The question is this: If healing is *guaranteed* in the atonement, why would Paul prescribe medicine instead of deliverance to Timothy? Here we find Timothy being commanded by the Apostle Paul, under the inspiration of the Holy Spirit, to take medicine. The present-day teachers of "God-guarantees-healing-for-all" would not approve of medicine as the recommended treatment for illness. Instead, they teach that having to take medicine is a sign of

85

weak faith. Here Paul is actually telling Timothy to take medicine, and just one chapter before this Paul tells Timothy to—

. . . set an example for the believers . . . in faith . . . *(1 Timothy 4:12).*

Apparently Paul considered it no contradiction to be an example of faith and still take medicine. Timothy was not rebuked for being sick, and he was not told to exercise more faith. He was told to *take medication,* and this would not conflict with his being an example of faith to believers.

If we are going to accept the Word of God uncompromisingly, let us accept the whole counsel of God. We have no right to add or subtract from His Word.

Job is an outstanding example of a man whom God accepted and blessed. He was pronounced blameless and upright, and God said that there was no one on earth like him *(Job 1:1,8; 2:3).*

When Satan was confronted by Job's impeccable record, he attacked Job's motives, accusing him of serving God out of selfishness. Satan challenged God to test Job, and God withdrew His protection. Then all of Job's possessions were taken away by Satan, with God's permission *(Job 1:12).*

Despite the heavy losses, Job did not sin, but instead worshiped God *(Job 1:20-22).* Satan then hurled the challenge that if Job were physically afflicted he would denounce God. Satan was given permission to inflict disease on Job *(Job 2:7).*

Here is the burden of the Book of Job. Job, a righteous man (declared so by God), is afflicted with disease when all evidence indicates that he should have received God's blessing.

Job's friends came to comfort him. To them the answer was simple: Men deserve what they get (chapter 4). Sin will receive God's curse and righteousness will receive God's blessing *(4:7-9)*. Since Job was suffering, it was obvious that God was punishing him.

These friends tried to make Job confess that he was a sinner and admit that he deserved his calamity. In the final chapter God steps in to denounce Job's comforters and uphold Job's integrity. His friends receive God's pardon only after Job intercedes for them *(Job 42:7,8)*.

The Book of Job teaches that man must not presume to sit in judgment upon another person or upon God, who does what man cannot comprehend *(Job 37:5)*.

To those who argue that God must heal every believer or else He is a Respecter of persons, I refer them to their own argument. *Matthew 8:16*, *12:15*, and *Acts 10:38* tell us that Jesus healed all who came to Him. This is used to establish that God is obligated to heal all or be guilty of showing favoritism.

This formula breaks down right where it begins. The Gospel record shows three incidents of Jesus raising the dead. Surely there were other candidates during Jesus' ministry, but *only three* were raised from the dead. Mark does not tell us that Jesus healed all who came to him in *Mark 1:34*. We are told instead that

Jesus healed "many." A great multitude of "impotent folk" were at the pool of Bethesda, but only one man was healed by Jesus (*John 5*).

What shall we say to all this? There is healing for us, but this healing is a *benefit* and not a *guarantee.* God still heals today, but not all are healed.

Man does not have all the faculties to grasp the whole range of facts and be able to consider their relationship to each other. He cannot comprehend the scheme of the universe, much less the God who created him.

It is unscriptural and unspeakably cruel to tell a person already sick and flat on his back that his confession of sickness put him there.

I heard an evangelist say that a little boy died of an incurable disease because his parents prayed, "Thy will be done". This evangelist said that the parents were responsible for their son's death. This is not only unchristian, but inhuman. There is not a shred of Scriptural evidence to make the claim that praying "Thy will be done" will result in negative results.

The parents of another child suffering with an incurable blood disease were encouraged by a minister to make positive confessions, claim their son's healing, and refuse to acknowledge the child's illness.

When their son died they were spiritually destroyed. The minister shrugged off the whole affair with, "They let down on their faith." Job said it well: "Miserable comforters are ye all."

Sure, there are sicknesses that continue because of a lack of faith, *but not every sickness.* Yes, there are some situations that can be remedied with a positive confession, *but not every situation.* Yes, God heals people today, *but not all are healed.*

To simplify complex problems without Scriptural support is to present false doctrines that lead people into agony.

I know some sinners who are enjoying marvelous health while I can name some sincere Christians who are suffering from chronic ailments.

What right do we have of imposing guilt and condemnation on top of an already-difficult burden? Why should we become ''Job's comforters''? It is the better part of wisdom to ''weep with those who weep'' *(Romans 12:15 NASB).* We have every right to pray a positive, uplifting prayer of faith for a fellow brother who is sick. We have no right to condemn.

Some Good Christian Sense

I have, on numerous occasions, come across Christians who claimed someone else's healing with a positiveness and assertiveness that commanded attention. I wondered to myself if they would be as bold about their own confession of faith if it had been their own incurable cancer.

One man in particular was lying in bed with cancer. He had been reduced to skin and bones. A Christian sister came to visit him while I was there. She prayed for him and then turned to me and said, ''He is healed. There's nothing to worry about. God said it in His Word and it has to be true.''

89

One week later the man was dead. Our assertive sister had by this time already told the immediate family and quite a few church members that the man was healed.

Now this leaves me somewhat perplexed. I suspect that this woman's faith was nothing but presumption. The psalmist prayed to be kept from presumptous sins *(Psalm 19:13)*. This is a good prayer for all of us!

What right have we to declare a person healed without a direct word from the Lord? We should pray with a positive attitude because the New Testament always supports that kind of praying, but we have no right to declare a person healed when we do not have a word from God.

We have no right to tell someone to throw away his medicine. Let the person who is thanking God for his healing go to his doctor and get his clean bill of health, and then throw away the medicine with the doctor's approval. By this the Lord not only receives glory from the person healed, but his healing becomes a testimony to the doctor.

Suppose someone came to me and wanted to pray for my eyesight. I wear glasses, and if I were to take them off, 80 percent of the scenery would vanish. Suppose after prayer I was told to take off my glasses, and as an act of faith step on the rims and crush them as I claim my healing. I take off my glasses immediately a blur takes over. It is obvious to me that I have not been healed. I state this fact and am told not to worry about anything. I am told that the blurred vision is only a "lying symptom." All I have to do is claim my healing.

To that I would respond, "Well, let's go to lunch; I'll drive." I grab my keys and fumble for the door. On my way out of the office I say, "Just steer me in the direction of the parking lot." By this time my faith-generating friend is getting a little concerned. I assure him I can detect my car because it is white. I get to the parking lot, put the key in the door lock, and discover that it is the wrong car.

Finally I get to my car. We get in and I notice my faith partner buckling his seat belt. I rev up the engine and take off, narrowly missing a fire hydrant and proceeding through a stop sign. By this time my faith partner is going to be mumbling prayers and crossing his fingers as his knees start to bypass each other.

You see, if someone is going to take the responsibility of telling me to crush my eyeglasses and trust in God, he ought to take the responsibility of driving with me in my car.

This article appeared in the Orange County *Register*, July 23, 1979, by Paul Levine, J.D. Copley Syndicate, based on a 1979 Pennsylvania case:

> Trusting God to cure him, Herbert makes his wife promise that she won't give him insulin for his diabetes. She hides the medication and would not give it to him, even when he became seriously ill. Herbert dies two day later and the state charges his wife with manslaughter.

The court found the wife guilty because she had the legal duty to help her husband, regardless of his wishes. She should have called for medical assistance when her husband became critically ill.

To tell someone to get rid of his medication and trust God for a healing is to invite a lawsuit. We do not have the right to practice medicine without a license, nor are we required to do so.

Jesus told a leper after healing him to show himself to the priest. Since the priest declared him unclean, the priest would have to declare him clean and allow him to come back into society *(Mark 1:40-44)*. This is a sensible method for testing our healing.

A Christian brother came into my office one day, and in the course of our discussion told me he did not believe in doctors and would never take medicine. He said that Jesus was the divine Physician. I told him that if this was his personal conviction he had every right to it.

Romans 14 tells us we can have personal convictions. But I cautioned my brother that his personal convictions did not permit him to look at another Christian who visited the doctor and took medication as any less a Christian.

So whatever you believe about these things keep between yourself and God *(Romans 14:22)*

We are not to use our personal convictions as a yardstick to measure someone else's spirituality:

Who are you to judge someone else's servant? To his own master he stands or falls. And he will stand, for the Lord is able to make him stand.

You, then, why do you judge your brother? Or why do you look down on your brother? For we will all stand before God's judgement seat.

So then each of us will give an account of himself to God *(Romans 14:4,10,12)*.

Why some people are healed and others are not is a mystery. But healing is not the only mystery we face.

The Mystery Of God's Deliverance

The Word of God declares on numerous occasions that God will deliver his children. The following is a short list of such promises: *Psalms 46, 91, Isaiah 50:2; Jeremiah 1:8, 39:17; Daniel 3:17; Romans 8:21.*

The Scriptures describe the deliverance of Lot *(Genesis 14, 19)*, Moses *(Exodus 2)*, and Israel *(Exodus 14)*.

Daniel, Shadrach, Meshach, and Abednego were delivered in *Daniel 3:19-28* and *6:22*. The apostles testify of their deliverance in *Acts 5:19; 12:7; 16:26; 2 Timothy 4:17*.

When Peter was taken to prison along with the other apostles, an angel came at night and opened the prison doors, letting them out *(Acts 5:17-20)*.

93

When Peter was taken to prison, the angel of the Lord appeared the day before Peter's execution and released Peter *(Acts 12)*. When Paul and Silas were taken to prison at Philippi, God delivered them by sending an earthquake (Acts 16).

These Scripture passages may cause some people to assume that God always delivers His children, and that God must deliver His children or He would be guilty of showing favoritism. However, we need to examine the Scriptures further. In *Acts 21*, Paul was again taken to jail. A series of trials brought him to Rome as a prisoner. This time there was no earthquake to bring deliverance. Paul died.

In *Acts 12* we discover that before Peter was imprisoned, Herod placed James in jail. But James was not miraculously delivered. James was killed with the sword.

In *Acts 7*, Stephen was not miraculously delivered from a hail of stones. We cannot conclude that Stephen was denied deliverance because he lacked sufficient faith. The Word says:

Now Stephen, a man full of God's grace and power, did great wonders and miraculous signs among the people *(Acts 6:8)*.

Just moments before his martyrdom, the Word tells us, Stephen was *full of the Holy Spirit* and experienced a revelation of Jesus standing beside God the Father *(Acts 7:55)*. If there was something wrong with Stephen's faith, let the same thing be wrong with my faith!

The Scriptures teach that God will deliver us. When I am in trouble I go to the Lord for deliverance. But there may be times when I will not receive the deliverance I desire. When and if this happens, I must not walk away dejected, as if something is wrong with my faith or there is necessarily some secret sin. This would not only put me in condemnation, but would overlook some of the other valid reasons for not being delivered, reasons that, although they are beyond my understanding, are nevertheless valid. Jesus gave Peter a valid reason for a situation in which he would not be delivered:

> I tell you the truth, when you were younger you dressed yourself and went where you wanted; but when you are old you will stretch out your hands, and someone else will dress you and lead you where you do not want to go. Jesus said this to indicate the kind of death by which Peter would glorify God *(John 21:18,19)*.

Someone might object, what glory would the death of a saint bring to God? I do not know, but I can read, and that is what is says. Peter was called to die for God's glory.

We also read that others will suffer for God's glory. It was God who said that Paul was not only chosen to carry His message far and wide but would "suffer for my name" *(Acts 9:15,16)*.

The writer of Hebrews tells us that many faith-heroes received God's deliverance

(Hebrews 11:32-34). However, he goes on to inform us that—

> . . . Others were tortured and refused to be released, so that they might gain a better resurrection. Some faced jeers and flogging, while still others were chained and put in prison. They were stoned; they were sawed in two; they were put to death by the sword. They went about in sheepskins and goatskins, destitute, persecuted and mistreated—the world was not worthy of them. They wandered in deserts and mountains, and in caves and holes in the ground. These were all commended for their faith, yet none of them received what had been promised. God had planned something better for us, so that only together with us would they be made perfect. *(Hebrews 11:35-40).*

If sickness should come, my response will be, "I know there is healing in the Word. I know the Lord has made provision for my healing." I will go before the Lord and ask for His healing touch. But if that healing does not come immediately, I will not go away saying that my faith is to blame or that there must be some secret sin, unless the Holy Spirit indicates this to me.

There is a mystery associated with God's deliverance and healing, and I will not presume to bridge these mysteries with pat little answers.

Elisha was one of the all-time Old Testament

greats, but he suffered from an illness from which he died *(2 Kings 13:14)*. Can I conclude that Elisha got sick and died because he lacked faith? If this is my conclusion, I need someone to explain *2 Kings 13:20,21* to me.

Elisha was buried in a sepulcher. Some time later, while Moabites were invading the land, soldiers wishing to bury one of their comrades quickly placed the dead man into Elisha's sepulcher. When this dead man was let down and touched the bones of Elisha he was brought back to life and stood up on his feet.

Does this sound like the Elisha who got sick and died because he lacked faith?

Some might argue that Elisha lived under the Old Testament economy and did not have the New Testament promises of healing. To this I disagree. Elisha had the promise of Exodus 15:26, which promised God's healing:

I am the Lord who heals you.

He had the promise of *Exodus 23:25*, which announced that sickness would be removed from us. He had the promise of *Deuteronomy 7:15*, in which Moses preached that the Lord would take away all sickness. Elisha had dozens of promises in God's Word. He did not have to live in the New Testament dispensation to qualify for healing.

What shall we say to all this? The ways of God are not always understood by us. There are mysteries about healing and deliverance that we cannot fathom.

Healing, like deliverance, is not a *guarantee*

but a *benefit* of Calvary. Being redeemed from the curse of the law does not guarantee that one will never get sick.

If a person gets sick he should go to the Lord for healing. There is healing in the name of Jesus. Multiplied thousands will testify to God's healing of incurable diseases.

I have seen "incurable" cases of cancer respond to the power of Jesus' name. I have received many testimonials from people who, while worshiping the Lord in our congregation, were healed. I know of many instances where people have come to the altar for prayer without the thought of praying for their healing. The power of God moved upon them and they walked away healed.

I can find no reason for Naaman the leper being healed other than God producing his healing. Naaman, captain of the Syrian army, was a leper. He did not serve the Lord God and was probably actively involved in raiding Israeli territory. Someone could have protested God's desire to heal Naaman, pointing out the fact that he was an uncircumcised heathen and that there were many lepers in Israel who needed healing.

God does as God desires because God is sovereign. We cannot accuse God of playing favorites. He is Lord. He does not have to discuss His moves with us. With our matchbox brains we could never comprehend the vast and limitless wisdom of God. No matter how spiritual we become, we are still the clay and He is still the Potter.

7
POSITIVE CONFESSIONS AND GOD'S WILL

Accounts of people claiming blessings and making "positive confessions of faith" are rapidly growing in the wake of faith teachers who declare that the only thing standing between us and an overcoming Christian life is exercising our faith through positive confessions.

Well-meaning people who want to reach out for all that God has for them are willing to try this seemingly simple exercise. But the testimonials are not always encouraging. Take this account given to me by a sincere Christian young lady.

It was a busy morning and I was running late. I arrived at Los Angeles International Airport to find it congested as usual. If I hurried I could catch my plane to Chicago. I finally found a parking space on the fourth level of the parking lot, quickly gathered my baggage, locked the car door, and started for the elevator. I was about thirty feet from the car when I felt my car might be broken into and I should move it. I stopped, turned around, and looked at my car. For one brief moment the message of a faith teacher flashed across my mind. I had been taught that if I used my faith, the Lord would protect me. I prayed and asked the Lord to protect my car and not let anyone break into it. I prayed in Jesus' name, turned around, and headed for my plane. I had all the confidence and assurance that my car was safer in that lot than it would have been in my home garage.

I was away two weeks, and during that time I thanked the Lord for the opportunity to use my faith, and I rejoiced that in His name we were protected from evil.

When I arrived back in Los Angeles and saw my car, I was numb. The side window of the car had been pried open, the car was unlocked, things in the glove compartment were scattered around, and my adding machine was stolen.

It was a long, thoughtful drive home.

Faith teachers tell us that the Bible method for gaining victory is by speaking out our faith. One of their key passages of Scripture is Mark 11:23,24:

I tell you the truth, if anyone says to this mountain, ''Go, throw yourself into the sea," and does not doubt in his heart but believes that what he says will happen, it will be done for him. Therefore I tell you, whatever you ask for in prayer, believe that you have received it, and it will be yours.

What We Say is What We Get?

At first reading it may seem that all I need to do is to speak to my mountain. Speaking out my faith is what I am told will make things happen in my life. Miracles are waiting for me to speak them into existence. But is it true that what we say is what we get? Did Jesus really teach this?

In Matthew 12:34 Jesus said that the heart is the power behind the tongue. The heart plays a vital role in my faith. Jesus qualifies speaking to my mountain with ". . . shall not doubt in his heart." Real creative power comes not from the mouth with words but from the heart through faith. The heart is the all-important issue.

Suppose I asked a contractor to build a triple-level mansion for me. I describe in detail the Spanish tile roof, the winding driveway, the swimming pool, and the tennis court. When the contractor asks me for the blueprints, I hand him a set of plans for a ramshackle, tumbledown shed. The contractor takes my plans and builds accordingly.

I can stand up and verbalize a lot of positive confessions, but if my heart has stamped on it the blueprints of doubt, my heart's *attitude* and not my *words* will be reproduced. If my mouth

101

is speaking victory but my heart is brooding in defeat, my greatest need is to change the attitude of my heart—not the words that come forth from my mouth. The heart's energy is much more powerful than the tongue's words. Our words are not magic, nor are they creative in themselves. We can actually make a positive confession with our mouth and at the same time be out of fellowship with God.

These people come near to me with their mouth and honor me with their lips, but their hearts are far from me *(Isaiah 29:13)*.

A positive confession of faith can be just so much sham and nonsense. Jesus teaches that what I do is more important than what I say. My calling Him Lord and not doing what the Lord demands of me is a contradiction *(Luke 6:46)*.

Faith without works is dead. Balance is essential; without it I can look pretty foolish. James points this out clearly.

Suppose a brother or sister is without clothes and daily food. If one of you says to him, "Go, I wish you well; keep warm and well-fed," but does nothing about his physical needs, what good is it? *(James 2:15,16)*.

To stand up and make a positive confession, "Be warmed and filled" is worthless unless we accompany that positive word with positive action. Can you imagine the good Samaritan on the Jericho road coming across a bleeding man who was ambushed by thieves, and saying something positive like "Be ye bandaged "? That situation calls for good *works* as well as good *words*.

Check The Context

The theology of positive confessions has been built up on passages of Scripture that do not have the remotest connection to positive confessions. A text without a context can become a pretext.

I have not only read but listened to faith teachers continually repeat a passage from Proverbs 6.

> ...you have been trapped by what you said, ensnared by the words of your mouth *(Proverbs 6:2)*.

The implication is that if you make negative confessions you will be snared by those words. But this is not the context of the verse at all. Instead, Solomon is warning people not to be hasty in cosigning for another person's debt because if the debt is not paid you become liable. Using Scripture out of context to support teaching is not only unethical but misleading to Christians who have not studied the Word.

Another favorite text used by faith teachers is Isaiah 45:11. The King James Version translates it this way;

> Thus saith the Lord, the Holy One of Israel, and His Maker: Ask me of things to come concerning my sons, and concerning the work of my hands command ye me.

103

At first glance this verse certainly seems to encourage us to speak our mind, and that God will then bring it to pass. This text seems to be telling us to let God know what it is we want, and He will do it. In fact some faith teachers go so far as to say that God isn't going to do *anything* for us unless we speak out the command.

Now let's look at the context. Israel is in exile but God promises to raise up a heathen king to deliver them. The prophet Isaiah uses the analogy of the potter and the clay. He says that the clay cannot tell the potter what to do *(Isaiah 45:9)*. The clay has no right to criticize the potter. In like manner, the Lord has the right to do as He pleases. Isaiah 45:11 does not encourage us to command God to do anything. The prophet is actually saying, "How dare anyone attempt to tell the Creator what to do?"

Why can't we see that in the text ? What we actually have in Isaiah 45:11 is an idiom meaning "commit something to the care of someone else." God is asking the Jews to commit their circumstances into His hands because He is capable.

The New International Version puts it this way:

> This is what the Lord says—the Holy One of Israel, and its Maker: Concerning things to come, do you question me about my children, or give me orders about the work of my hands?

The Dead Sea Scrolls preserves the original text:

> Thus says the Lord, the Holy One of Israel,

who fashions the future, Will you question me concerning my sons, and concerning the work [of my hands] command me?

So this passage teaches the exact opposite of what the faith teachers are teaching. This passage does not encourage us to command God. For a layman not to study the context is understandable, but for a minister of the gospel who has an obligation to preach the uncompromising Word of God, this is inexcusable.

What Should I Confess?

Joshua was told, before he led the children of Israel into the Promised Land, that God would be with him: "As I was with Moses, so I will be with you" *(Joshua 1:5)*. Based on the promise that God made to Joshua, what if Joshua had tried to cross the Jordan River in the same way that Moses crossed the Red Sea? What if he had held his staff over the Jordan waiting for it to divide? God's plan for Joshua was different. He was to have the priests march into the Jordan first, and then the waters would divide. Just because God did something one way for one man in the past is no guarantee that He will do it the same way for me.

Joshua witnessed the walls of Jericho tumble down by the power of a positive shout. But suppose he had tried to use this method in his strategy for taking over the other cities? He would have failed. God's specific word to Joshua for Jericho cannot be turned into a formula. Suppose Naaman, who was healed of leprosy

105

by dipping in the Jordan River seven times, would have invited other lepers to come to the Holy Land and dip in the Jordan? Would they also have been healed? God's specific word to Naaman cannot be used as a formula for healing others.

I walked through a theater, already in escrow to become X-rated, and then placed my hand on the building, praying that we would get it for the work of the Lord. We miraculously received that theater and have been worshiping in it ever since. But this miracle and the way we received it cannot become a pattern for receiving other things. How do I know this? I know it because I also laid hands on another building, praying that we might receive it to expand our work. But we never received the building I claimed. In fact, our fellowship purchased a building that we did *not* claim. God works in His own marvelous ways, and we cannot turn God's dealings into a simple formula of positive confessions.

I have no right to try to walk on water just because Peter did. I cannot insist that God is showing favoritism if He allows Peter to walk on water and not me. God does what He wants to do. Neither can I take the instruction that Jesus gave to the rich young ruler to sell all that he had and make it a universal prescription for everyone to follow.

There are limitations in God's Word when it comes to applying it to our lives. It would be presumptuous for a Christian to walk into a lion's den demanding that God shut the lion's mouths because He delivered Daniel in a similar circumstance. Unless God specifically tells us to do something, we are on dangerous ground trying to force God's hand with a positive confession.

Negative Confessions

If too much has been made of the positive confession, it is also true that an overemphasis has been made of the negative confession. We are told never to say such things as "I am catching a cold" or "I think I'm getting a headache" because these negative confessions will actually produce the malady. We are told to affirm the positive even when it is a contradiction to reality. As a result, many Christians are afraid to admit they have a cold or an allergy. One young man who was sneezing refused to admit he had an allergy even though all the symptoms were present. This carries overtones of the mind sciences.

Christian Science teaches that disease is only an illusion. Any evidence of disease is considered false regardless of the symptoms. Mrs. Fillmore, cofounder of Unity, taught that as a child of God she did not inherit sickness.

Pain, sickness, poverty, old age and death are not real, and they have no power over me. There is nothing in all the universe for me to fear (*Lessons in Truth*).

Mrs. Fillmore denied that she could inherit disease, sickness, ignorance, or any mental limitations whatsoever. The roots of the positive and negative confession teaching are imbedded in the soil of the mind sciences.

107

Consider for a moment the negative confessions you may have made in the past that never materialized. When I first dated my wife I doubted that she would ever agree to marry me, but we have been happily married for over 16 years. I have been sick several times and did not have the faith to believe I would be healed, but I was healed and am healthy today. I must admit that what I say is not always what I get. My words are not magic.

Teaching people that the words they say will come to pass is building a theology of fear and bondage. Telling Christians that they should never use expressions like "I'm tickled to death" or "I'm dying to know" because they are negative and may hurt us is nothing short of ridiculous. I know a man who, during moments of frustration, says, "I'm a monkey's uncle." Does that present the possibility that he might bring it to pass? Hardly.

Once during a very hectic week in which my wife had to travel with me to quite a few appointments, she said, "Joe, you are driving me crazy." Should I be looking for signs that Nancy is going off the deep end because of this negative confession of faith?

When I look through my Bible I find many negative confessions of faith. Somebody should have told Paul to use a more positive approach when he testified:

We are fools for Christ, but you are so wise in Christ! We are weak, but you are strong! You are honored, we are dishonored! To this very hour we go hungry and thirsty, we are in rags, we are brutally treated, we are homeless...When we are slandered, we answer kindly. Up to this moment we have become the scum of the earth, the refuse of the world *(1 Corinthians 4:10,11,13)*.

Paul would have been called on the carpet by some faith preachers for making this negative confession of faith in 1 Corinthians. He said that the outward man was wasting away, yet inwardly we are being renewed *(2 Corinthians 4:16)*. No faith teacher would feel comfortable standing before his congregation and declaring, as did the Apostle Paul:

That is why, for Christ's sake, I delight in weaknesses, in insults, in hardships, in persecutions, in difficulties. For when I am weak, then I am strong *(2 Corinthians 12:10)*.

This teaching of refraining from any negative statements has kept many Christians from going to the Lord in prayer and unburdening their heart for fear that they would be making a negative confession to God in prayer. How utterly unscriptural! What tragic bondage!

Someone should have explained to James that negative confessions were unscriptural, because he actually encouraged Christians to confess their faults to each other *(James 5:16)*. James went on to teach that this negative confession would actually result in physical healing!

109

Positive Confessions, Negative Results

One Christian young lady refused to accept her pregnancy, insisting that God had promised her no more children. Evidences of her pregnancy were considered, "lying symptoms." This was a test of her faith, and she would remain steadfast, believing God despite the evidence.

But she was pregnant, and nine months later what she considered to be lying symptoms was having its diapers changed. Fortunately for her, the child, though delivered in her home, was a healthy baby.

A minister friend of mine confided in me that his wife was caught up in faith teaching. For years she desired to raise a family but could not become pregnant. She attended a faith-teaching service, went to the altar for prayer, and was told by the minister to claim her pregnancy and use 1 Samuel as her text.

She "acted on the Word" by going home and decorating a room for her soon-to-be-born baby. She bought baby furniture and prepared for this child, all the while "claiming" she was pregnant. It has been over three years and she is still claiming she is pregnant.

There is an obvious error here that needs correcting. How do we know what to claim? How do we know God's will in a particular matter?

God's Will

There are many things about God's will that we can say we know. We know that it is God's will for everyone to be saved. We know that it is

110

God's will that everyone who is saved be baptized in water, study His Word, pray, and put away malice, envy, jealousy, pride, and lying; this is God's general will for His people.

But many faith teachers have embarked on a teaching program that would have us believe we can be just as sure about God's will in specific matters.

They argue that they always know God's will because they know God's Word. But since when have we arrived with all the knowledge we need concerning God's will? No one, including the faith teachers, always knows God's will in every matter. Not even the person who has totally memorized God's Word can make that claim.

Paul certainly did not claim to know God's will in all matters. In 1 Corinthians 4:19 he says, "I will come to you very soon, if the Lord is willing."

Acts 16:6-10 gives us a clear example of Paul not knowing God's specific will:

Paul and his companions traveled throughout the region of Phrygia and Galatia, having been kept by the Holy Spirit from preaching the word in the province of Asia. When they came to the border of Mysia, they tried to enter Bithynia, but the Spirit of Jesus would not allow them to. So they passed by Mysia and went down to Troas. During the night Paul had a vision of a man of Macedonia standing and begging him, "Come over to Macedonia

111

and help us." After Paul had seen the vision, we got ready at once to leave for Macedonia, concluding that God had called us to preach the gospel to them.

Paul thought he was in God's will when he attempted to preach in Asia, but the Holy Spirit blocked that opportunity. Paul then attempted to preach in Bithynia, but the Holy Spirit prevented that outreach too. It is obvious that Paul did not know the Lord's will specifically here. He knew he was called to preach, but God had to redirect his steps geographically.

In Acts 18 Paul refused to stay at Ephesus but said he would return if it was God's will *(Acts 18:20,21)*.

Someone could have complained, "Paul, can't you be a little more sure of yourself? You are encouraging other Christians to go around saying, 'If it be God's will.' That's not very positive, is it?"

When it comes to God's general will for the Body of Christ, we have a clear word. When it comes to God's specific will for us in daily matters, we need to wait on the Lord.

What's Wrong With If?

When the leper came to Jesus he said to Him, "If you are willing, you can make me clean" *(Mark 1:40)*. That was his prayer.

Suppose some high-powered faith preacher had overheard the leper. He might have reprimanded him. "Mister, you should never say 'if' to Jesus. When you use 'if' in your praying

112

you don't know whether it's God's will or not. That prayer is doomed to failure. It is a negative confession.'' Then with an air of confidence he might have turned to the Lord and said, ''Isn't that right, Lord?'' But Mark tells us:

> Filled with compassion, Jesus reached out His hand and touched the man. ''I am willing,'' he said. ''Be clean!'' *(Mark 1:41).*

Jesus did not criticize the leper by saying, ''Don't ever use 'if' when you come to me. If you use the word 'if' you are going to get negative results. Polish your request and come back when it's a little more positive.''

Jesus did not say that this man's theology was bad, because there is nothing wrong with saying, ''Lord, if it is Your will, heal me.'' He did not question Jesus' *ability*; he questioned Jesus' *will*.

The man with the epileptic son in Mark 9:22 questioned Jesus' *ability* when he said, ''Lord, if you can do anything, take pity on us.'' It is always wrong to doubt God's ability. But the leper in Mark 1 was not questioning God's *ability* but His *will*.

The greatest prayer ever prayed was prayed by Jesus in the Garden of Gethsemane. He said, ''Not my will but Thine be done.'' Those who say that Jesus prayed that prayer once so that we would never have to say ''If it be Thy will'' had better check things out with James, who said:

> ...you ought to say, ''If it is the Lord's will, we will live and do this or that'' *(James 4:15).*

113

The If Test

There are some "if" tests that our prayers need to pass. Jesus gives us one such test in John 15:7,8:

> If you remain in me and my words remain in you, ask whatever you wish, and it will be given you. This is to my Father's glory, that you bear much fruit, showing yourselves to be my disciples.

Since there seems to be a strong aversion to using the word "if" in connection with a positive confession, I draw your attention to the "if" that Jesus used in verse 7. Jesus qualified my asking whatever I wanted with the word "if"—if I abide in Him and if His words abide in me. My requests need to pass this "if" test. It is not a matter of my simply asking for whatever I want. Jesus said that His Word must first be inside me. This is a safety factor to keep me from asking for foolish things, as we shall see.

If I were carrying a bowl of soup and someone bumped into me, what would spill out ? Obviously, soup would spill out. If a sponge is filled with water and it is squeezed, what drips out of the sponge? Obviously, water comes out. If I have Jesus' words abiding in me and I ask the Father for something, what words are going to come out? Jesus' words! If I fill up with Jesus' words *(Colossians 3:16)*, then Jesus' words will come out. What goes in must come out.

If we use John 15:7,8 to mean that I can go out and claim four Cadillacs, one for each

114

direction, with built-in swimming pools and color TV sets, and turn this into a materialistic grab bag, we need to read the passage over again. There is nothing wrong with prosperity, but this passage is not our go-ahead to storm heaven for material blessings. John 15:8 tells us, "This is to my Father's glory, that you bear much fruit, showing yourselves to be my disciples." What fruit? Converts *(Romans 1:13)*, the fruit of the Spirit *(Galatians 5:22,23)*; the fruits of righteousness *(Romans 6:21,22)*. Jesus is talking kingdom business here. He is referring to our character, our conduct, and our service.

The Lord will meet our needs, insofar as meeting our needs will in turn be used to meet *His* needs. God will equip me with everything I need to get His business done. Money is no problem. Whatever it is I need to get His work accomplished, God will supply it. I believe it! But becoming a Christian is not a materialistic free-for-all to cater to my greed and build my own kingdom. John 15:7 is an "if" test to which I must submit my requests and desires.

Perhaps someone will object to the use of an "if." To them it may sound like a cop-out. If it is, then Jesus and John must go on trial, because they used the word "if".

This is the assurance we have in approaching God: that if we ask anything according to his will, he hears us. And if we know that he hears us—whatever we ask—we know that we have what we asked of Him *(1 John 5:14,15)*.

115

There is the "if" again—"If we ask anything according to His will." This tells me that if I ask for something outside God's will, it will not be given with His approval. Why would God give me something that will hurt me?

When my son, Joey, was two years old he wanted a pocket knife. He asked for it, but it was not according to my will, and therefore, he did not get it.

Our Will And God's Will

God's will is not always our will, and whenever there is a disagreement here, God's will should be upheld. If God had answered my prayers according to my will I would have been a cowboy riding with Hopalong Cassidy, the Cisco Kid, and Fuzzy Jones. Our will keeps on changing. It is tainted and nearsighted.

Isaac's will was to bless Esau. God's will was to bless Jacob. Peter's will was for Jesus to avoid going to Jerusalem at all costs. If it had been up to Peter, there would have been no Calvary.

Mary and Martha wanted Jesus to leave the stone in place at Lazarus' tomb, since Lazarus had been dead four days. God's will was to call Lazarus back from the dead.

Our will so often falls short of God's will. It makes sense to remind ourselves, "If we ask anything according to his will, he hears us" *(1 John 5:14)*.

I am a little suspicious of those who brazenly declare that they always know God's will. They point to the Word and say, "I always pray in

God's will.'' It's so cut and dried! They will tell you, ''The Word says, With his stripes we are healed'' *(Isaiah 53:5)*. ''The Word says, He forgives all my sins and heals all my diseases'' *(Psalm 103:3)*. ''The Word says, They will place their hands on sick people, and they will get well'' *(Mark 16:18)*. Then they will say, ''If a child of God is sick, it is always God's will for him to be well. All we need to do is claim that healing.''

If I were sick I would be first in line to get my healing. I don't relish the idea of being sick. I believe in the healing power of Jesus. I witnessed a young lady come to the altar for prayer who had a tumerous growth on her wrist, and while she was praying the tumor vanished right before our eyes.

My mother prayed all night in a hospital room while her grandchild was in an oxygen tent with spinal meningitis. The next morning that girl did not have a trace of this problem. Yes, I am a firm believer in God's power. But I want you to know that I see something in Scripture that will not support the ''everybody-must-get-healed'' teaching. Healing is not a *guarantee* but a *benefit* of Calvary. If we are going to accept the teaching that Christians would never get sick if they exercised a positive confession of faith, and that every Christian who is sick should always be healed, what are we going to do with the Scripture passages that will not support that teaching?

We do not always know what God's will is in every situation. If Paul knew what God's will

117

was for his thorn in the flesh, he would not have asked God to remove it three times. God refused:

> "My grace is sufficient for you, for my power is made perfect in weakness." Therefore I will boast all the more gladly about my weaknesses, so that Christ's power may rest on me *(2 Corinthians 12:9)*.

We do not always know what God's specific will is for us in every situation. When the three Hebrew young men stood before King Nebuchadnezzar and refused to bow to his gold-plated image, they made a positive confession of faith *(Daniel 3:17)*.

> If we are thrown into the blazing furnace, the God we serve is able to save us from it, and he will rescue us from your hand, O King.

Now that is as positive as you can get. But I want you to notice the next verse: "But even if He does not."

Now that ruined a perfectly good confession of faith. This would have scandalized many of today's faith teachers. Why did they insert that negative, "But even if He does not"? It was because they did not know exactly how God was going to work! We do not always know the will of God and how it will be accomplished. We must beware of being so sure of what heaven is up to that we begin to boast about

118

things of which we know very little *(James 4:15,16)*.

We Can Be Dead Wrong

The children of Israel attacked the Philistines and were soundly defeated. They regrouped and declared that they would take the ark of the Lord and go out against the Philistines *(1 Samuel 4)*. They called for the ark because past victories were won this way *(Joshua 6)*. Surely they were standing on the Word by sending for the ark of the Lord! They even had Scripture to back them up!

> When the ark of the Lord's covenant came into the camp, all Israel raised such a great shout that the ground shook *(1 Samuel 4:5)*.

They brought the ark of the Lord the way Joshua did at Jericho. They shouted the way Israel shouted at Jericho. The Philistines heard this "positive confession of faith" and were afraid *(1 Samuel 4:7)*, just like the people of Jericho were afraid.

Israel could have said, "We know the will of God in this matter." They could have said, "We are following the Word." But Israel lost the battle miserably. Their confession was bold, but all it amounted to was a lot of noise as far as God's will was concerned.

God's will is the all-important factor. He sees the complete picture. We are so often like the nearsighted turtle that falls in love with an army helmet. As difficult as it is for us to

119

concede, God has a better overall understanding of things.

When God saw Gideon hiding behind a winepress, He saw what our eyes would have never detected, and He sent an angel to inform Gideon of what He saw. The angel said, ''The Lord is with you, mighty warrior'' *(Judges 6:12)*.

Gideon certainly did not believe he was a mighty warrior. But God sees what we cannot possibly see. When we pray, ''Lord, not my will but Thine be done,'' we are turning all heaven's power loose within us.

Gideon's will would be, ''Lord, keep me from being detected by the Midianites.'' God's will was to pit Gideon and 300 men against the entire Midianite army and to deliver Israel from seven years of oppression. God's will is far superior to ours. He is able to do immeasurably more than we can ask or imagine *(Ephesians 3:20)*.

It makes sense for us to pray for God's will to be done. Jesus looked at Peter and saw not a reed, but a rock. When I realize that God may be seeing something in me that surpasses my fondest dream, I say, ''Lord, have Thine own way.''

When I look into the Word and discover who I am spiritually in Christ, I develop a greater confidence. I begin to see an emerging picture of what God sees in me. Then my confession of faith centers around what God sees in me:

I am heir of God *(Romans 8:17)*. I know that everything will work together for good *(Romans 8:28)*. And I am more than a

120

conqueror, able to face any set of circumstances and come out victoriously
(Romans 8:37).

These promises and more are the basis of my
positive confession of faith. There are so many
promises in God's Word for me that are
legitimately mine that I do not need to lay claim
on things that God's Word will not support.

8
DISTORTING THE TRUTH

Remember the strange-looking mirrors at amusement parks? They looked like they had melted in the sun. They sagged in the middle or at the bottom, and when you stood in front of one you got a distorted image of yourself. One mirror made you look as if your head were stretched like a rubber band while the rest of your body was packed into a blob. Another mirror made your head look like an elephant had walked over it while your body looked stretched out of proportion. These mirrors were designed to distort your image.

As long as the distortion is in the mirror it's funny and everyone has a good laugh. However, when the distortion is in our mind, it's not so funny.

Truth can be stretched out of proportion until it is distorted. The results can be dangerous, as I have seen over and over again by people who have come to me for counseling.

123

Recently a retired nurse (we'll call her Edith) came into my office to tell me about a close call she had with death. Edith loves the Lord and has been walking in the ways of the Lord for many years. She experienced God's healing touch when she developed heart trouble several years ago and was miraculously healed. This last year she had been diagnosed a diabetic, but with a proper diet she was able to control her problem. Being an active person, she became tired of the restrictive diet and prayed that the Lord would heal her as He did her heart condition. At about that time she had been listening to a faith teacher over the radio who urged his listeners to claim their healing, confess deliverance with their mouth, and live a healthy, medicine-free life.

Edith was convinced that this is what she should do. In an act of faith, she made her confession of healing and felt free to eat the restricted foods.

After several months she noticed very clear evidence that the symptoms were manifesting themselves again. As a registered nurse she knew the symptoms and consequences. The nausea, night sweats, blurred vision, weakness, and loss of concentration returned. In desperation Edith called out to God and redoubled her efforts at claiming her healing. The symptoms increased until she was forced to go to a doctor. Fortunately, she was saved.

Having been Edith's pastor for five years, I can testify to her sincerity and love for the Lord.

124

What happened to Edith?

Her desire for healing and the teaching that she could simply claim it with her mouth led her to believe she could force a healing to take place. But we cannot force God's hand through positive confession or any other kind of confession.

Two teenage girls in Korea traveling to a church service in another village came to a turbulent stream. They decided to trust God and walk across this swift current because the Gospel records that Peter walked on water.

They had faith in God to help them or they would never have stepped into the stream. Two days later their dead bodies were pulled out of the river.

Yes, Jesus told Peter to get out of the boat and come to Him. But taking that Scriptural account and making it apply to those girls and their situation was distorting the truth, since the Lord did not specifically command *them* to cross the stream.

Many tragedies and near-tragedies have been created by people making positive confessions.

Just the other day a lady called me. She was in tears as she tried to make sense out of what she had just been told by a counselor at a Christian TV station.

She was told by a well-meaning Christian counselor that the reason she was not healed was because she lacked faith for her healing. She was told that if a burglar came into her home to rob her and she had a gun to defend herself and didn't use it, it would be her fault

125

because she had the means of defending herself.

This was applied to her desire for healing. She was told by this counselor that she had the means to be healed (positive confession of faith), and that if she didn't use it, it was her fault that she was sick.

When she called me she said that the guilt and frustration laid on her was worse than the sickness she had been experiencing.

Someone needs to come to grips with these frustrations and distortions of the truth. Too many of God's children are being tortured by so-called servants of God and their advice.

The Book of Job is a classic example of this kind of distortion. Job was no ordinary man. He enjoyed a prosperity that few men on earth had in his day. The Bible says that he was the greatest man in his part of the world *(Job 1:3)*, an impressive character reference. God's opinion of Job is especially fascinating because the Lord expressed His view of Job to Satan:

> Have you considered my servant Job? There is no one on earth like him; he is blameless and upright, a man who fears God and shuns evil *(Job 1:8)*.

God's view of Job should have carried weight. However, Satan had another point of view and insisted that Job's righteousness was a front for his desire to keep God's blessing, and that he served God merely for profit. Satan said that Job would curse God to His face if God withdrew His blessings.

Satan was permitted to test his theory.

Calamities befell Job in rapid succession *(Job 1:13-19)*, until he had lost all his cherished possessions, including his children.

Contrary to Satan's belief, Job fell down and worshiped God *(Job 1:20-22)*. This reaction underscored his tremendous faith in God and Satan's erroneous view. Satan, unwilling to concede failure, pressed his controversy further and suggested that Job would curse God if he was afflicted in his body. God again granted permission, and when we next look, Job is in great pain.

Satan even tried to use Job's wife to encourage him to curse God. But the record states that Job did not sin in what he said *(Job 2:10)*.

News of Job's affliction spread far and wide, and three of his friends came to visit. What follows for the next 34 chapters is a raging controversy between Job and his friends. This unique battle of words gives us a clear insight into the theology of Job and his friends.

A very interesting parallel is seen between what Job's friends believed and what many faith teachers are sharing with their followers today.

The following is a summary of Job's friends' theology.

Eliphaz the Temanite stated that innocent and righteous people never suffer. Since Job was suffering, it was obvious that God was punishing him for some wickedness *(Job 4:7,8; 5:17; 15:20)*.

Bildad the Shuhite added this bit of circular reasoning to Eliphaz's views: If Job

127

was upright God would have prospered him, but since Job was suffering, it was obvious that Job was evil *(Job 8:6)*.

Zophar the Naamathite had harsh words too. He decided that God was actually being lenient with Job. Job was not getting all that his iniquity deserved *(Job 11:6)*.

Suffering was irrefutable evidence to these three men that a person was living under the curse of God's judgement. They even took the liberty of cataloging Job's supposed sins.

. . . you must have refused to loan money to needy friends unless they gave you all their clothing as a pledge—yes, you must have stripped them to the bone. You must have refused water to the thirsty and bread to the starving. You sent widows away without helping them, and broke the arms of orphans. That is why you are surrounded by traps and sudden fears . . . *(Job 22:6-10 TLB)*.

Their theology is summarized as follows:

Major Premise: God blesses the righteous and punishes the unrighteous.

Minor Premise: Job is suffering affliction.

Conclusion: Job is unrighteous and is being punished by God.

Job's response to his friends' "theology" was "Miserable comforters are ye all" *(Job 16:2 KJV)*.

128

Job disagreed with their oversimplification. He stated that some wicked people prosper *(Job 12:6)*. He observed that some wicked people live to a ripe old age, increase in power, and are safe and free from fear. The correction of God is not evident in their lives *(Job 21:7-9)*.

Job goes on to say that these wicked people have many children, were happy, spend their years in prosperity, and go to the grave in peace *(Job 21:11-13)*. Job's observations are identical to those of Jeremiah the prophet, who at one time registered a complaint with God that the wicked were prospering *(Jeremiah 12:1)*.

Other men of God saw this discrepancy too. Solomon wrote:

> In this silly life I have seen everything, including the fact that some of the good die young and some of the wicked live on and on *(Ecclesiastes 7:15 TLB)*.

Although Job's arguments were based on an observable fact, his defense went unheeded while his friends became more and more insistent. They believed that some sin in Job's life could explain his suffering.

Finally Eliphaz offered Job advice that sounds so much like the advice of today's faith teachers. He told Job:

1) If you will get into the Word you will become prosperous.
2) If you will get into the Word your prayers will be answered.
3) If you will get into the Word you will be

129

able to decree a thing and it will be
established.
4) If you will get into the Word your
positive confessions of faith will lift up the
downcast *(Job 22:21-28)*.

What was Job's reply to their advice?
I have not departed from the commands of
his lips; I have treasured the words of his
mouth more than my daily bread *(Job
23:12)*.

Despite his loyalty to the Word, Job says that
God still allowed him to suffer *(Job 23:12-17)*.
During this ordeal there was no one to come
to Job's defense or present his case. Heaven's
silence magnified Job's suffering.
Job's friends took this silence as an
endorsement of their theology and became
relentless in their efforts to persuade Job to turn
from his sin so that God would again prosper
him. They insisted that his suffering was proof
that he had failed to live up to God's Word and
that he therefore should repent *(Job 36:11-21)*.
Whose theology was correct—Job's who
believed that God tried the righteous with purpose *(Job 23:10)*, or Job's friends', who believed
that anyone who was suffering was experiencing God's punishment?
In chapter 42 the Lord thunders His verdict:

I am angry with you and your two friends,
because you have not spoken of me what is
right, as my servant Job has *(Job 42:7)*.

God accepted Job's theology and rejected his friends'.

Some faith ministers teach that Job brought his sickness and tragedy upon himself, because he states:

What I feared has come upon me; what I dreaded has happened to me *(Job 3:25)*.

They say this *negative confession of faith* is responsible for all the tragedy that befell Job. If that is true, why didn't God let Job know this so that he would avoid doing it again? How could Job be left in the dark about something so critical to his well-being? Why didn't the Lord give credit to Job's comforters, who stated clearly that Job's problem was his own fault? Instead, the Lord tells them that their opinion of Job is wrong and that Job's opinion is correct. If God said that Job was approved, that is the final word. We cannot add to God's evaluation of Job.

Lastly, if Job's negative confession was responsible for his suffering, and if God is no Respecter of persons, then David should have experienced the same tragic results when he said—

One of these days I will be destroyed by the hand of Saul *(1 Samuel 27:1)*.

But David did not perish by the hand of Saul or the hand of any other person. David's negative confession of faith did not result in his death. There has been entirely too much em-

131

phasis on positive and negative confessions of faith.

What conclusion can we draw from the account of Job in the light of the rest of God's Word?

First of all, we can say with assurance that the righteous may suffer for reasons other than sin and a lack of faith. James lists Job as someone who suffered because of his *righteousness*—not his unrighteousness:

> Brothers, as an example of patience in the face of suffering, take the prophets who spoke in the name of the Lord. As you know, we consider blessed those who have perservered. You have heard of Job's perseverance and have seen what the Lord finally brought about. The Lord is full of compassion and mercy *(James 5:10,11)*.

The prophets seem to have suffered because of a *positive* confession, not a negative confession. These men were commended for their perseverance in waiting out the ordeal until God delivered them. They were not chided for failing to claim immediate deliverance. Their suffering was the result of their righteousness.

Secondly, Job teaches us that God did not will Job's sickness and that God did not will Job's financial ruin. God *permitted* these circumstances when He accepted Satan's challenge, but He did not *will* Job's calamities.

News came to Job on one occasion that "the fire of God fell from the sky and burned up the sheep and the servants" *(Job 1:16)*. Now it

132

could have seemed to Job as if God were engineering these tragedies, but we know from Scripture that it was *Satan* who produced and directed them.

However, God *permitted* these severe trials to touch Job's life. God was fully aware of what was happening, but He stood by while this test was in progress.

Many faith teachers insist that God would never do such a thing, but if we believe the *whole* counsel of God we cannot sidestep the fact that God will at times use physical suffering for His purposes.

There are too many impressive passages in the New Testament that contradict what faith teachers want us to believe. They state that some suffering, although not engineered by God, will be used to bring Him glory.

I realize that this line of teaching runs counter to the Wall Street version of the gospel, which allows for no pain or cross-bearing. I can almost hear the protests and objections.

That God would receive glory from my misfortune is a difficult concept to understand. I will not pretend to understand it. I certainly would not seek suffering, and I would be the last in line to sign up for a refresher course in pain in order to bring God glory. I have a natural aversion to pain. But how can we get around the references that teach that God in some instances receives glory from saints who are suffering?

Jesus said that one man was born blind *(John 9:1-3)* not because of sin but in order that "the

133

work of God might be displayed in his life." Jesus said of Lazarus *(John 11:1-4)* that his sickness would bring glory to the Son of God.

Some might argue that these two men were *delivered* by the Lord, and that their deliverances, rather than their suffering, brought glory to God. If this is true, then I still need someone to explain *John 21:18,19*. For in this passage we are told that Peter would die for the gospel and that his death would glorify God.

The Lord told Ananias that Saul, the new convert to Christianity, would suffer many things for the name of the Lord *(Acts 9:16)*.

Paul founded the church in Galatia because of sickness *(Galatians 4:13,14)*. That sickness resulted in glory to God.

To the teachers who declare that every redeemed child of God should be wealthy and healthy, and that if they are not it is because they are living under the curse of the law, I submit the historical record of Paul.

It would be much easier if we had only to explain why the ungodly suffer. We can easily explain the consequences of sin. We can easily explain why curses would come upon those who do wrong. But the task becomes difficult when it comes to explaining why the righteous suffer. Why do the godly get into accidents, lose loved ones, experience financial reversals, and suffer tragedies?

We certainly do not have Scriptural justification to tell all these saints that there is sin in the camp.

The problem with this faith-teaching

134

theology is that, although it looks good on paper, it does not fit either the revealed Word of God or human experience, and is nothing more than the theology of Job's comforters.

Like Job, many saints who are suffering do not need *condemnation* but *comfort.* It takes inhumane cruelty for a minister to say—

Poor Mrs. Brown—she died of cancer. If only she had faith to believe God, she would have been healed.

Who would dare tell Mrs. Brown's children that? What right have we to even suggest that to Mr. Brown?

That kind of callous explanation is not only cruel and unchristian, but all too often "Poor Mrs. Brown" has more faith in God than the minister who passed judgment on her.

How are we to minister to those who are suffering like the Jobs and the Mrs. Browns?

God ruled out the approach of Job's friends, who told Job that his suffering was his own fault. They punctuated their arguments with accusing fingers and condemnation.

Are we to tell our suffering brothers that if they had more faith they would not be suffering? Dare we suggest that they take a crash course in positive confessions?

The Corinthian Christians developed a theology that came dangerously close to Job's comforters. They were enjoying a measure of peace and prosperity and began interpreting their pleasant circumstances as the result of their greater revelation. They were beginning to get "puffed up" with their blessings and to look down on those who were less fortunate. Paul leveled stinging sarcasm at them to correct this dangerous shift.

> Already you have all you want! Already you have become rich! You have become kings . . . To this very hour we go hungry and thirsty, we are in rags, we are brutally treated, we are homeless *(1 Corinthians 4:8,11)*.

The contrast is vivid: While these Corinthian Christians were full and rich and reigning, Paul was hungry, poor, and reviled. While they enjoyed prosperity, Paul endured persecution.

How are we to interpret this set of circumstances? How are we to explain their prosperity and Paul's poverty? Would we dare suggest that Paul's faith was inferior? Would we argue that the Corinthian Christians must have had a greater and more fuller revelation, a stronger faith and a superior grasp of God? How are we to interpret their prosperity and Paul's poverty? How are we to explain Paul's suffering? The way we explain Paul's suffering will determine how we minister to those who are suffering.

The Apostle Paul had to explain the problem of suffering to the Christians at Thessalonica.

> . . . so that no one would be unsettled by these trials. You know quite well that we were destined for them. In fact, when we were with you, we kept telling you that we

would be persecuted. And it turned out that way, as you well know *(1 Thessalonians 3:3,4)*.

Paul had no difficulty in explaining his present suffering or the suffering of other Christians.

The Corinthians, on the other hand, were becoming puffed up in their prosperity. Paul warned them against this and said he was sending Timothy, who would remind them of the teaching of Jesus, which Paul taught "everywhere in every church" *(1 Corinthians 4:17)*.

What we need is a gospel that can be preached everywhere and in every church, and not just in some isolated area on earth where fair circumstances and abundance exist. We need a gospel that works everywhere.

I am afraid that the Wall Street gospel is designed to work for the full, the rich, and the reigning. It cannot minister to the Ethiopian who is being persecuted for Jesus' name. Any gospel engineered for the healthy and wealthy cannot be preached in nations where hundreds of thousands are suffering persecution, go hungry and thirsty, and are homeless *(1 Corinthians 4:11)*.

The faith teachers who proclaim the gospel of prosperity cannot preach in Russia, where to believe in the Lord Jesus means being blacklisted from all the important jobs.

What we need and what Paul preached is a gospel that works "everywhere in and every

137

church''—a gospel for the both the poor and the prosperous, a gospel for those suffering as well as for those enjoying peace. If it doesn't work as effectively in the Congo as it does in Chicago, it isn't the gospel Paul preached.

How are we to minister to the suffering church? While touring Rome several years ago, I visited the Roman Coliseum, where Christian gladiators fought against each other and against wild beasts before the bloodthirsty crowds. The Coliseum is empty now, but if you look across the decaying arena you can imagine the tens of thousands of Romans waiting for the next event of bloodshed.

I imagined as I stood there that if I could push the clock back 2000 years, I would suddenly be in trouble. As a Christian I would run the risk of being captured and brought to this arena, not as a spectator but as one more bit of amusement for the crowds. I would be chained up in one of those underground cells waiting for my summons to face a wild animal. The thought brought shivers. Imagine the fear, the absolute horror one would experience as he was about to be devoured by a lion.

How would we comfort those who waited in line in chains, as they slowly moved toward the doorway that opened into the arena? What would we tell them? Could we dare walk among those who were condemned, announcing that if they only had more faith they wouldn't be there? They were there *because* of their tremendous faith! Or who would dare suggest that these Christians who were consigned to face the

138

lions were there because of some secret sin?

While in Rome I also visited the catacombs—600 miles of endless tunnels under the city of Rome, used by Christians of the first several centuries to hide during the persecution.

These catacombs were also used as the burial place for Christians. When these graves were opened, the skeletons told the horrible story of persecution. Heads were found severed from the body. Ribs and shoulder blades broken. Other bones were found badly burned. Little children as well as adults suffered the awful persecution and were buried there. The Christian graves were marked by symbols etched in the walls. There were harps, anchors, and crowns, but most often the symbol of the fish could be seen.

I wonder how a modern-day faith teacher would comfort those who returned to the catacombs with the remains of their loved ones. I wonder what word of consolation they would offer those who were burying their loved ones. Would they tell the father who was burying his little daughter that she would still be alive if he knew how to make a positive confession of faith? Would they have the audacity to say that he should have claimed deliverance and exercised faith? Would he be told that his daughter died in vain?

Nero, the insane Roman emperor, had the city of Rome burned while he played his fiddle on the palace roof, and then he blamed the fire on the Christians.

A massive persecution swept the Roman empire. Christians were killed and tortured by the thousands. *Foxe's Book of Martyrs* describes the awful deaths. Some were put into leather bags with serpents and scorpions and thrown into the sea. Others were covered with wax and hoisted on poles and used as torches to light Nero's gardens.

How are we to explain these tragic persecutions? How are we to minister to those who suffered during them?

In America we are surrounded by peace and protected by nuclear missiles. We are living in a sea of abundance. We are full, rich, and reigning, just like the Corinthians. We must not make the mistake of thinking that we have all this because we are superior, or have a deeper revelation, or exercise more faith. We are not more spiritual than our suffering brethren. Once we realize this, we can minister to them properly.

Peter teaches us how to minister to the Jobs and Mrs. Browns who are suffering.

And the God of all grace, who called you to his eternal glory in Christ, after you have suffered a little while, will himself restore you and make you strong, firm and steadfast. To him be the power forever and ever. Amen (*1 Peter 5:10,11*).

We are to tell our suffering brother that he is *called*. His suffering does not lessen his spirituality with God. He needs to hear that no one can touch his eternal reward. We dare not become so materialistic that we forget the greatest treasure we possess—eternal life. We

140

need to comfort our brother with the words, ''Brother, your suffering is only for a little while. No one and nothing can touch your eternal reward.''

And we need to tell him that despite his feelings, despite the circumstances, there is *purpose* in it. That is what Peter said to the suffering church, and that is what we need to say to the suffering saint. There is purpose in it. God will use it just as He uses blessings—to perfect you. God is not punishing, but God is using this suffering to ''perfect, strengthen, and settle you.''

And even in this we can say, as Peter, ''To Him be power forever and ever, Amen.''

This is how we are to minister to the suffering. Distort this truth and we will hear what Job's friends heard from God—

I am angry with you . . . you have not spoken of me what is right, as my servant Job has *(Job 42:7).*

SUMMARY

The Word of God is not opposed to prosperity. But we can be sure that God is more interested in the person behind the wheel than the make of the car being driven.

To place material possessions in a prominent position not only incites greed but is as foreign to the New Testament as camels on Wall Street. Jesus said that a man's life does not consist in the abundance of possessions. To say that God "wills" material prosperity for all His children is to say that any child of God not enjoying prosperity is outside God's will and is living a Satan-defeated life. This is not Biblical.

God did not design this planet to accommodate disease, pain, poverty, and suffering, but man's sin has put this planet under a curse. The manifestation of that curse is everywhere. We are not placed in a bubble of protection that keeps us from the rain that falls on the just and the unjust *(Matthew 5:45)*. Which Old Testament or New Testament saint fits the image of an invulnerable superman untouched by the hurts and sorrows of this world? Not even Jesus escaped the pain. We have not been promised smooth sailing. Our guarantee is a safe landing.

The Scriptures make it abundantly clear that God's will is not always what we would have ordered. His will may at times run contrary to mine. It may even bring hurt, and during those times my consolation is found in the promise:

For our light and momentary troubles are achieving for us an eternal glory that far outweight them all *(2 Corinthians 4:27)*.

Abraham's long wait for a promised child, Joseph's jail sentence, Moses' wilderness wait, and Paul's suffering for the sake of the gospel must have seemed needless at the time. Surely there must have been an easier way. But we cannot rush the harvest. The seed that falls into the ground does not produce overnight. The process of becoming holy is not instant.

God's will and God's way is not always the way I would plan things. If God has scheduled me to be second-string punt-returner on His team, I must stop frustrating myself by demanding that I play first-string quarter-back. If God's will is for me to be first-string quarter-back, I will not please Him or fulfill my mission by playing any other position. He knows what He is doing and where I best fit in.

I have no right to declare God's will for any matter without a word from the Lord. While on a ship caught in a violent storm, Paul waited many days after fasting and praying before he stood up to speak. He spoke only after he heard from heaven *(Acts 27:21-26)*. Suppose at the first sign of trouble Paul had jumped up and made a positive confession of faith: "Gentlemen, I claim the safe landing of this ship. Not one board will be broken and all the cargo will be saved." That would have been a positive confession based on God's general promise to deliver us out of trouble, but it would have been presumptuous, because the ship broke apart and the cargo was lost. We are authorized to claim only what God inspires us to claim. God's Word will keep us from becoming ashamed.

143

We have been victimized by our culture. The American obsession with success, shortcuts, and pleasure has created an Americanized gospel—a perverted gospel that teaches "Ye shall know them by their Cadillacs." When we stand before the Holy Trinity, our possessions won't amount to a hill of beans, and the fruit that Jesus will be looking for will be the results of our obedience to His will. Jesus is Lord. I cannot make Him my servant.